THE
SUCCESSFUL
AUTHOR
MINDSET

A HANDBOOK FOR SURVIVING
THE WRITER'S JOURNEY

Joanna Penn

First edition

The Successful Author Mindset:
A Handbook for Surviving the Writer's Journey

First Edition (2016)

Copyright © Joanna Penn (2016).

ISBN: 978-1-912105-59-5

Requests to publish work from this book should be sent to:
joanna@CurlUpPress.com

Cover and Interior Design: JD Smith

Printed by Lightning Source

www.CurlUpPress.com

Contents

Dedicated to my Mum, Jacqui Penn, for her unfailing positivity throughout my upbringing. My can-do attitude and proactive mindset stem from her belief in me, and her support of my journey.

I love you, Mum.

"If you can change your mind,
you can change your life."

William James

Why this book?

The act of writing and creating words on the page is an inherently lonely thing. Sure, there are writers' groups and communities online and off, but when actually writing, you're alone with your own mind, and that can be the most difficult thing.

Even if there's no one criticizing you externally, you still have that voice inside that tells you how terrible your words are, how you will never make anything of yourself creatively, how pitiful your attempts are at creation. You battle negative thoughts and the ebbs and flows of writing energy.

And it seems like you're alone.

But in fact, all of us who write are bobbing around in this ocean of creativity, going through the same issues. I feel the same way you do, and as I started to talk about my own thoughts and feelings around writing, I found many others going through the same things, even experienced authors who had been writing for over forty years. I discovered that I wasn't alone.

So this book collects the mindset issues that writers go through, that I have been through myself over the last nine years, and that perhaps you will experience yourself at different times on the author's journey. These words are an attempt to help you understand that what you're going through is normal and to be expected as part of the creative process.

Each small chapter tackles a possible issue and then offers an antidote, so that you can dip in and out over time. It's not a craft book on how to write, and there's no information on publishing, book marketing or making money as a writer. I cover those topics in other books. This is purely about the emotional rollercoaster of being a writer and how to deal with those issues along the way. I've included excerpts from my personal journals over the years and quotes from well-known writers so you can see how universal these aspects are to the creative process, even if not all of the book is relevant to you right now.

The book is broken down into sections:

Part 1 goes through the potential issues you may face during the creative process of writing.

Part 2 tackles what happens after you publish and as you move through the author journey into successive books.

Part 3 offers some tips for successfully managing your author mindset in order to foster a long-term creative career.

This has not been an easy book to write, because I bare my creative soul in these pages, but I hope that it helps you understand that you're not alone.

Part 1: Mindset Aspects of Creativity and Writing

1.1 Self-doubt and imposter syndrome

"Bad writers tend to have self-confidence,
while the good ones tend to have self-doubt."

Charles Bukowski

A few years ago, I went to ThrillerFest in New York to hear some of the biggest authors in the industry speak. One panel featured R.L. Stine, who has sold over 400 million books, Lee Child of Jack Reacher fame, and David Morrell, who created the character of Rambo. It also included one of my own writing heroes, Clive Cussler, who sat next to Sandra Brown, a romantic suspense author with over 36 New York Times bestsellers. Collectively, the authors on the panel had sold over 600 million books and had been translated into 35 languages. They were at the pinnacle of writing success and it was both intimidating and inspiring to hear them all speak.

After a great panel discussion packed with anecdotes, one member of the audience put her hand up.

"I'm a new writer," she said. "I'm halfway through my manuscript and I feel like it's terrible. I'm doubting my story. My writing sucks. I think I should just throw it all away because it's so bad."

These mega-successful authors all nodded and smiled at her with recognition on their faces. Then, one by one, they spoke of their own self-doubt.

"Even after making the bestseller lists so many times," said Sandra Brown, "I feel like I'm a fraud and that this time everyone will find out."

David Morrell talked about reading his words from yesterday, the words he thought were amazing at the time, only to find they were terrible … and how that happens most days.

They went along the panel and every single one of those authors, some of whom have been writing for over forty years, said they all suffered from various aspects of self-doubt.

This comforted me because, like everyone else in the room, I feel waves of self-doubt on a regular basis. It comes through if I second-guess my first draft writing and let my internal editor start work before I finish the draft. It gets particularly bad when I am about to publish a novel or when I'm asked to speak or give an interview about my fiction. It gets especially bad at writing conferences when I can't help but compare myself to other authors. (More on comparisonitis later!).

Here's an excerpt from my journal in February 2011, on the launch of my first novel.

"I was going to have launch drinks but I cancelled them. I feel like weeping. I'm tired, disappointed, wondering what the hell I'm doing with my time. I have a total loss of self-confidence now my words are out there. I know I should live in the moment and be happy and celebrate finishing a book, but I'm anxious about people reading my thoughts as well as about how my Amazon rankings are. I feel that I'm being judged and found wanting."

My journals are full of passages like that. Those of you who read my books and listen to my podcast might not realize it, though, because I tend to keep my fears and insecurities inside the pages of my private writing. But now I'm being open about it because I realize that we're all the same.

To take it even further, imposter syndrome is an extension of self-doubt. It's the feeling that, despite the number of books written and the levels of achievement reached, we are frauds just pretending to be writers. Amazingly, this seems to be more common amongst the most successful authors. Imposter syndrome is rife in the author community, hidden by a veil of 'keeping up appearances.'

So, if you meet an author who seems a little distant or stand-offish, chances are that they feel like someone is about to discover that they are just a bag of jangled nerves. They are waiting to be found out and cast back into the darkness.

It seems that wherever we are on the writer's journey, self-doubt will come along for the ride.

Antidote:

Embrace self-doubt as part of the creative process. Be encouraged by the fact that virtually all other creatives, including your writing heroes, feel it too with every book they write. In fact, if you don't feel any kind of doubt, there's probably something wrong! And if you've reached the heights of imposter syndrome, you're probably doing pretty well in your writing career.

When you feel that creeping self-doubt, acknowledge it. Write down your feelings in your journal … and then continue with your writing.

If you're suffering badly, by all means talk to your writing community about how you feel. But I think there is a shelf life for this kind of confession from writers. Other authors and readers may be sympathetic if you share occasionally, but a writer who constantly talks about their self-doubt may erode the reader's confidence over time. So take a deep breath and get back to the blank page.

> "Do you need someone to make you a
> paper badge with the word 'WRITER' on it
> before you can believe you are one?"
>
> *Stephen King, On Writing*

1.2 Need for validation

"There is a deep longing to feel legitimate in the world, to feel that others hold us in regard."

Cheryl Strayed

I want my writing to move you. I want my voice to be heard and my story to be told. I want you to tell me that my book is great, that I am a good writer, so that I can stand proudly alongside my peers. I want recognition and I need validation for the hours I have slaved over this manuscript.

Someone please tell me that I am worth something.

Do you resonate with this?

It's at the heart of why I write. Perhaps it just comes down to "Please notice me. Please love me." In a crazy busy world, it can be hard to feel seen, to know that you are heard, and writing becomes a way to make even a tiny dent in the universe. Once our words go out from us, we want someone to receive them. That's why most writers don't write for money or fame, they write from this longing to share what's in their hearts.

After writing, this need for validation can spill into publishing decisions.

Am I good enough to get an agent and a publisher?

Am I good enough to be read and loved by readers?

Am I good enough to win prizes and thrill critics?

Am I good enough to sell millions of books, get fantastic reviews and to make a living with my writing?

Ultimately, this need for validation is what makes writers so desperate to get an agent and a publishing deal, and then so grateful when they are picked up, even though *they* are the talent and their manuscript is valuable.

It makes indie authors chase after the latest marketing fad, hoping that it will help them get noticed in a sea of books. It drives authors to read their own book reviews even though the good ones will puff you up and the bad ones will bring you down, and ultimately, they are just someone else's opinion.

Antidote:

This need to be heard, for validation and ultimately, love, will never go away. It's part of what drives us to write and to publish. We have to learn to harness that need in a way that sustains us rather than destroys us. We also have to learn to self-validate, to understand that the writing process is the point, rather than the reception of our work or the rewards that may or may not come. We need to nourish ourselves with the practice of creation and learn through experience that we are good enough, we are worthy, regardless of what happens when our words go out into the world.

Self-knowledge of this need for validation can also stop us from making decisions that may harm us in the long run. For example, an author who takes an average publishing advance of $10,000 for their book may have given up their intellectual property asset for the life of copyright and may never see another dollar from it. All because they wanted an agent to tell them they are a good writer, and they crave the validation of a publishing deal.

For indie authors, validation comes from sales and reviews from a growing readership. This need can turn into a constant rechecking for the latest reviews, with days ruined by a one-star review and obsessing over what could have been different.

The only antidote to all this is to keep writing.

"Measure your worth by the dedication to your path, not by your successes or failures."

Elizabeth Gilbert, Big Magic

1.3 Fear of failure

"I'm afraid of failing at whatever story I'm writing—that it won't come up for me, or that I won't be able to finish it."

Stephen King

Failure in writing means different things to different people, and the definition will change as you move through the writer's journey. Clearly, if Stephen King still suffers from fear of failure, then it will never go away and we're all in good company!

Fears are generally about yourself or about how others will receive your work. Here are some of the fears and thoughts that might come up around failure.

- I can't finish writing this book. I'm a failure before I've even started

- I finished my book, but I've failed to make it live up to what I wanted it to be

- I've failed to get an agent or a publisher

- What if no one buys my book and it fails to sell?

- What if my book gets terrible reviews?

- What if my friends and family hate it, or are offended or angry?

- What if it makes no money and I've wasted all this time and energy on something pointless?

Your definition of failure will also depend on what your goals are. As your career develops, the stakes may be higher, but equally the sense of failure can be deeper. I know authors who have had multi-six-figure publishing deals and then have felt a failure when the book didn't sell well enough to justify that advance. Others that had movie deals where the movie was never made, or even worse, was a flop. A new writer on their first book might consider getting any advance or even just a movie option to be fantastic, but our definition of success changes over time and so does the perception of what constitutes failure.

So what does this fear feel like?

The physical experience of fear hasn't changed since we were running away from predators and living in caves. Of course, if we 'fail' as writers, no one's going to die, but that doesn't change the physical manifestation of fear or anxiety.

Here's one of my own examples from public speaking, something that authors often have to do as they become more successful, and which is a very common fear around failure. Ultimately, you feel you might 'fail' because you won't be able to speak, or you'll make a mistake and people will think you're an idiot, or they will laugh (at you, rather than with you!)

"I was about to speak to over 300 people in a venue that was new to me, and there were people in the audience that I wanted to impress. Ten minutes before my talk, I went to the bathroom for the third time, my stomach churning. I took a couple of painkillers to stop the stress headache getting worse. I sprayed on extra deodorant, as I was sweating more than is considered lady-like. My mouth was dry so I kept sipping water, exacerbating the need for the bathroom. My heart pounded in my chest as I redid my makeup. I took some deep breaths and walked back to the conference center, singing in my head to psyche myself up. I smiled and walked up on stage."

I am pretty confident these days speaking as a non-fiction author, but ask me to read a passage of my own fiction aloud and I crumble. I still tend to refuse, as the fear is so great, something I need to tackle as my own career progresses.

The physical experience of fear or chronic anxiety can include:

- Stomach pain, nausea, diarrhea and frequent urination

- Excess sweating

- Heart thumping and pulse pounding, vision may narrow

- Headache, feeling faint, shortness of breath

- Problems sleeping, repetitive negative thoughts

Not a lot of fun!

If you're getting these symptoms all the time, then definitely see a professional. But if you experience them as part of your author journey when you come up against situations you fear, I'd say this is entirely normal. Some anxiety is a reality in any part of life, and so you have to find ways to deal with it.

Antidote:

The experience of fear is often worse than the actual event and if you are never afraid as a writer, then you are never challenging yourself. No one will die because you received a scathing review, or the only person who reads your book is your Mum, or you speak at a festival and people walk out.

Instead, consider what's the best that can happen if you go through whatever it is.

Think about the reward beyond the fear.

People might love your book. You attract new readers. You get paid for your creativity. Awesome!

It's also a good idea to reframe the fear. Because, actually, no one really cares what you're up to. People are bound up in their own worlds and the gossip will move on within a few days, whatever happens.

You can't expect the writer's journey to always be trending up. Like life in general, there will be highs and lows, failures and successes. Get past the fear and back to the writing.

"You only fail if you stop writing."

Ray Bradbury

1.4 Fear of rejection and criticism

"To avoid criticism say nothing, do nothing, be nothing."

Aristotle

Here's an excerpt from my journal, Jan 2011, just before I published my first novel.

"I'm scared of criticism. I want praise. I want everyone to like me and my book. That's why I'm scared of bad reviews and cruel comments. I don't think I can take them. What if I never write again because of something someone says? What if my book actually is bad? What if the criticism is true? Sometimes I wonder if it would be better if no one ever read my work, because then no one would attack me."

Even though I had a lot of support from my family during the process, there were still comments that hurt:

"Why can't you write something more like <famous literary writer>?"

"Why can't you write something nice that I can tell my friends about?"

Clearly I did go on and publish, but this fear is still very real.

There are many levels of criticism and rejection that we face as writers. They may come from:

- Writer's groups and other authors

- Editors, agents and proofreaders

- Family, friends and people we love

- Critics, reviewers, bloggers and people on social media

- Readers through bad reviews or even just lack of sales, which is a kind of rejection in itself

We identify with our work, so we feel that rejection of the book is essentially rejection of us as people. As Gustave Flaubert said, "We serve up a portion of our gut and the critics get the knives out." You may have bared your soul in your book and, of course, it reveals something about you. Criticism will always hurt because you care about your work.

Of course, there are times when rejection and criticism can be useful:

- **Rejection by an agent or a publisher** who is not a good fit for your book is a blessing in disguise because you may find a home for it elsewhere or happily self-publish later.

- **Constructive criticism by an editor** will improve your book and, however you choose to publish, I recommend using professional editors and proof-readers for all your books. It is the best way to make your book the best it can be and you don't pay an editor to praise your writing, so expect constructive criticism that will make your book better.

- **One or two-star reviews** hurt (so I generally don't read them!) but if you have lots of four and five-star reviews, the one-stars will make your book sales page look more authentic. The top prize-winning and bestselling books always have a lot of bad as well as good reviews, so a range is to be expected if your book is read by many. Of course, if your book only has one or two-star reviews, then consider that feedback. You have either categorized the book incorrectly and you haven't met reader expectations, or it's not good enough so you need to take the book down and get another edit before re-publishing. But at least people are noticing your work if they are criticizing it. Silence can be much worse!

So, how do you know when criticism is valid or not? There are some times when you need to take note of comments and other times when you need to ignore them.

A good critic knows what they are talking about but also knows their limits. They are respectful, they give examples and they judge your work by the right criteria. For example, I would never take editorial feedback from a children's book specialist editor for my thrillers.

A bad critic doesn't give examples and they judge your book by incorrect criteria. For example, the literary critics who reviewed *50 Shades of Grey* were never the target audience for that book, and readers of erotic romance generally loved it.

"Hear criticism and weigh it against your inner truth."

Julia Cameron

Antidote:

Build up resilience and a thicker skin over time, because, as a creative, you will face criticism and rejection throughout your whole career. You're never going to please everyone, so be aware that if you put your work into the world, there will be comments you don't like.

When it comes, don't turn the criticism over and over in your mind. Don't focus on the negative or give it more energy. Try using mindfulness as a technique. Be aware of what you're feeling, observe your thinking, watch your mind in action. Focus on the moment and not the feelings and thoughts that are escalating in your brain. Stop the mental tapes running. Catch yourself before you spiral into despair!

Understand the importance of criticism from editors and beta-readers, which helps to improve your work. Yes, it hurts to receive editorial feedback but it gets easier with each book because you have evidence of improvement. When I get my edits back, I still take a deep breath before opening the document and I will only look at them when I am energized.

Never work on edits if you're tired!

If you get useful criticism on your work early, you will lessen your chances of rejection later. The criticism has to be high-quality though, and from the right people. I am personally wary of writers' groups, and don't belong to one. I prefer to pay for feedback from professionals rather than listen to comments from unpublished writers who might not even like my genre. Many writers' groups skew toward literary writing and may belittle genre writers, so be sure to find people writing within your genre. Be careful whose opinion you listen to.

The fear of criticism and rejection is often worse than the actual reality. After all, you can't stop people having their opinion of your book, or of you personally. You can only change your response to the situation and the way you handle things. For example, some writers don't read reviews, others read them and don't care, and I'm sure others are really hurt. I try to let them rest on me briefly and then slip off. I take feedback and consider it, weigh it, and then get back to writing what I love anyway.

A supportive community is important for weathering the storms of criticism and rejection. Join a group of people who are going through the same issues. I don't think I could have written even one novel without the encouragement of my blog and podcast community. (Thank you all!) I also recommend the Alliance of Independent Authors, which has a fantastic Facebook group where we share issues and what we learn.

For more on this topic, check out *Resilience: Facing Down Rejection and Criticism on the Road to Success* by Mark McGuinness, or check out the interview on the topic here: www.TheCreativePenn.com/resilience

"If you are remarkable, some people won't like you. Criticism comes to those who stand out."

Seth Godin

1.5 Your inner critic

"For me and most other writers I know, writing is not rapturous. In fact, the only way I can get anything written at all is to write really, really shitty first drafts. The first draft is the child's draft, where you let it all pour out and then let it romp all over the place, knowing that no one is going to see it and that you can shape it later."

Anne Lamott, Bird by Bird

The inner critic is the voice that tells you that your writing is terrible and will always be terrible. That you're not meant to write. That your sentences are pathetic, your story is something only a novice would write, that you have no imagination. That you'll never be as good as this writer, or never make as much money as that writer – so what's the point?

This inner critic can fuel our self-doubt and fear of failure and can even stop us writing altogether.

So how do you shut down that voice in order to get words on a page?

Antidote:

Recognize the thoughts

You need to identify those critical thoughts so they are not just running through your mind like black sand, squashing the life from you. Julia Cameron's idea of morning pages from *The Artist's Way* is one method for doing this. The idea is to write three pages longhand every day and let everything out, all your thoughts and feelings about the world, about your writing. In that way, you will recognize the negative thoughts and exorcize them on the page. Sure, they will come up again tomorrow – this isn't something that ever ends for creatives – but for today, you know what they are and you can move into writing. I do this by journaling, but often only write a few paragraphs. That is enough.

Another way is meditation. Sit and watch your thoughts, listen to them and identify that they are not you. They lose their power and you can get on with writing.

Tell your critic to relax for now

We need that critical voice during the self-editing part of the creative process but not in first draft writing, so tell your critic to please take a nap for now and that you will honor her later when her help is needed. You don't want to banish her completely, because that critical eye is impor-tant for improvement, you just want her to rest for now. I used to get angry and try to shut that part of me down. There are countless articles on silencing or removing that inner critic. But I try to be thankful now, and gentle. I talk to that part of my self, something like this.

Thank you for helping me to be critical in the editing process, but right now, I need some time to play and be creative. I need you to rest, but please come back when I'm done and you can help me with the next part.

This may sound weird, but talking to myself has become part of my creative ritual. I do it in my head so I don't look like a crazy person!

Start writing anyway

Put your butt in the chair and get some words on the page. You don't have to sit down to write 'the best book ever,' as your inner critic will slaughter that idea pretty fast! But you can sit down to write the few lines that are in your head, or just a little chapter on something. Don't make the event into something scary. Don't build your part up. You're just sitting down to write. What could be so threatening about that? Make it fun and your inner critic may not even notice that you're writing!

> "We are not our writing. Our writing is a moment moving through us."
>
> *Natalie Goldberg, Wild Mind*

1.6 Fear of judgment

"The moment that you feel that, just possibly, you're walking down the street naked, exposing too much of your heart and your mind and what exists on the inside, showing too much of yourself. That's the moment you may be starting to get it right."

Neil Gaiman

You can't write that. You can't think that. You can't imagine those things. You don't have permission to be that person, to publish these words. You're a good girl. What will people think of you?

That's my inner critic speaking as I wrote *Desecration*, the first book where I stopped self-censoring my writing. But I was petrified about people judging me for that book.

I've always been a good girl, a people-pleaser, and I want people to like me. I don't like conflict, I don't like arguing. I want people to think I'm doing the right thing. I always did well in exams, I went to Oxford University, I got a good corporate job and climbed the ladder. I always pay my taxes early! But being a good girl, or a good boy, can stop the creative muse from what it really wants to say.

So it was terrifying but also liberating to indulge my fascination with tattooing, body modification and medical history in *Desecration*. I tackled the forbidden through my characters and went deep into myself. Those currents swept me onto *Delirium* and *Deviance*, the next two books in the trilogy. I indulged the crazy and the taboo. (In my books, of course. My life is pretty tame!) It turns out that my stories are dark and twisty when I let my author voice run free, and I have to keep reminding myself not to self-censor when I come to the blank page.

Or I would just stay safe in the shallows.

Can you identify with this?

Now that I have given myself permission to let the raw side of me loose on the page, I'm finally finding my true voice. A friend told me soon after *Desecration* was published that I've changed since I've become a full-time writer. But I think it's just that the inner me is finally making it to the surface after years of suppression and conformity to what society expected of me. I'm done with taming the crazy.

Our most powerful writing comes from the subconscious, that part of the brain we access when we shut down that inner critic and just let the words come. Fear of judgment will shut that part down, and we have to learn to let it go. Yes, it's a risk, but it's the only way your work will sing.

We all have fears that we need to conquer as authors. Why do we write if not to tackle the fears that others look to us to conquer? So how do we tackle this fear of judgment?

Antidote:

Understand that the book is not you

When people judge your book, remember that they are not judging you as a person. I might write about ritual murder in an Egyptian tomb (*Ark of Blood*), but clearly that's not what I do in my real life! If you read my blog or listen to my podcast, you'll know I am unfailingly positive and generally very happy! We are all complex creatures and our work is merely one aspect of our character at a specific point in time.

The easiest way to deal with fear of judgment around one book is to write another book, because who we are right now changes and the next book is something else again. We morph as our work does, or vice versa. I find the fear of judgment lessens with every book I put out there, because I've moved on.

Be strong and steadfast but also surround yourself with people who understand you.

My husband is (fortunately) understanding of my desire to visit strange spots when we go on holiday. On a romantic weekend in Budapest, we spent our time at the House of Terror and the mass grave in the old Ghetto of the Synagogue. In Paris, it was the catacombs where the remains of six million people lie in macabre underground decorative crypts. Both of these experiences were turned into scenes in my ARKANE thrillers.

These macabre interests are part of me and once I began to acknowledge them, I found others who enjoy them too. I hope you can find like-minded people who support your research and career, even if it's not your family or friends. Chances are you can find a community online, whatever you're into.

Understand that embracing the shadow side is psychologically healthy

In Jungian psychology, the shadow is a critical part of our whole self. Life is not all sweetness and light and there is only a thin veneer of civilization over our ancient animal selves. Death and fear, violence and sex will always be part of our culture, so as writers it's important to embrace that and reflect it in our writing. When the things we fear are on the page, they have less power over us.

Consider using a pseudonym

If your fear of judgment is justified, then consider using a different name. Many erotica authors use pseudonyms to protect their identities, and it's definitely the way to go if fear is stopping you from writing at all. It can also be a way to expand into other brands without impacting your existing reputation or confusing/offending your audience e.g. a traditionally published literary author writing indie romances on the side, or a children's author writing horror.

"The reaction to your art does not belong to you – and that is the only sane way to create."

Elizabeth Gilbert, Big Magic

1.7 Perfectionism

> "Perfectionism is self-destructive simply because
> there's no such thing as perfect. Perfection is
> an unattainable goal."
>
> *Brené Brown*

"How do you know when the book is done?"

This is a question that many writers struggle with, and consequently some books can take many years to write because the writer keeps messing with sentences, searching in vain for just the right turn of phrase. After agonizing for weeks, changing back and forth, they finally settle on a sentence and move onto the next one, only to come back weeks later and begin more revisions.

The truth is that nothing is ever perfect.

Even if you hire three separate editors and use ten different proofreaders, you will still get an email from a reader pointing out a typo or an error.

Go pick up any bestselling book from a traditional publisher and scour it for typos. You will find them.

Go look at any prize-winning or bestselling book on Amazon and check the reviews. The more popular the book, the more issues people will find with it. There will never be a book that will satisfy everyone and that's fine. Not everyone will like your book and a couple of typos are not the end of the world.

Antidote:

Strive for excellence and follow a process that will ensure your book is the best it can be. Go through your own self-editing, then work with a professional editor, do the rewrites that will help the book and use a proofreader. You could even use a site like Wattpad.com where you can post chapters and get feedback from readers as you write. But make sure you set a deadline for your book, otherwise this editing process can also be a form of perfectionism!

Once you have been through a rigorous process with an end point, get that book into the world, however you choose to publish. If you feel the itch to edit yet again, be honest with yourself.

- Is another round of changes really going to make a substantial difference to this book?

- Would it be better to work on the next book instead of constantly reworking this one?

At some point you have to stop listening to your inner critic or the negative voices of others. Do your best and let the book out into the world. For anyone seriously struggling with this, I recommend *The Pursuit of Perfection and How it Harms Writers* by Kristine Kathryn Rusch.

Of course, the problem may also be deeper. Look at chapter 1.4 on fear of rejection and criticism, and 1.6 on fear of judgment if you just can't let your words go out there.

"Have no fear of perfection – you'll never reach it."

Salvador Dali

1.8 Writer's block and procrastination

"If you get stuck, get away from your desk. Take a walk, take a bath, go to sleep, make a pie, draw, listen to music, meditate, exercise; whatever you do, don't just stick there scowling at the problem. But don't make telephone calls or go to a party; if you do, other people's words will pour in where your lost words should be. Open a gap for them, create a space. Be patient."

Hilary Mantel

Most writers have struggled with getting the words on the page at some point. But writer's block is not a monolithic disease with one cause and one cure. The term is often used as a catch-all for a number of issues which have different causes and solutions. Some of the blocks are caused by fears, anxieties and your inner critic, as covered earlier, but here are some more examples of when you might find writing grinding to a halt.

If you're blocked as a new writer writing a first book

The 'block' at this point is generally not knowing how to write a book, so you end up flailing around and wasting time, feeling frustrated because you're not getting any-where. It's sometimes due to lack of ideas or how to string them together, but more often it's just a lack of knowledge.

It could be the desire to write a certain type of book, e.g. literary prize-winner, and just not being able to write anything like it. That was my fiction block for years. My Mum was an English teacher and I went to Oxford University, so I was raised within the literary establishment. I thought the only book I should try to write would be something that could enter the Man Booker Prize, or something like Umberto Eco's *The Name of the Rose*.

But actually, I love reading fast-paced thrillers and my guilty reading pleasure while doing English Literature at school was Clive Cussler's Dirk Pitt. I love watching Bond films and my favorite movie is Con Air. Once I realized that I was 'allowed' to write fun books that people would enjoy rather than take seriously, you couldn't stop me writing! My block was gone and I focused on learning how to write those types of books.

Antidote:

Ignore what you (or other people) think you *should* write, and look at your bookshelf. What do you love to read? What do you choose as a guilty pleasure? Be honest with yourself, even if you come from a literary background. What's fun for you?

Then go write that.

Read some books on how to write a book (preferably about the genre you want to write in). See the Bibliography for suggestions.

Join a local class with other people writing their first books. Do some timed writing sessions based on creative writing prompts.

If you're blocked during a book in the 'saggy middle'

The block here could be lack of ideas. Maybe you had a fantastic start to the book and you know the ending, but you don't know how to knit them together. It could also be boredom with the story and a general feeling that it's not worth writing (see 1.1 self-doubt). It's likely that you're procrastinating at this point, filling your time with things that don't lead to getting words on the page.

You might also find that you're trying to make the book too long, when the idea is suitable for something shorter.

Antidote:

Do some more research around your theme, setting or characters for fiction, or topic if it's non-fiction. Fill that creative well. Think of your mind as a pipe. You have to put things in the top for the ideas to come out the bottom, transformed.

Take a break. If I'm stuck in the middle of a chapter, or just feeling 'over it' with a book, I'll go for a walk. Fresh air cures many ills! But sometimes, if I've been working on something for an extended period of weeks or months, I'll need a bigger break. A few days away from the manuscript, or a few weeks' holiday, and you'll come back to the page renewed.

But if you're really just procrastinating, stop what you're doing, get your butt into the chair and get writing. It's about doing the work!

If you're blocked after finishing a book when you think you should immediately start another one

Here's an excerpt from my journal a week after finishing *Gates of Hell*, my fifth full-length novel:

"My mind is completely empty. I will never have another idea. What if this book is the last one I ever write? What if I never have any more ideas? My whole life is now bound up in writing books and being an author. If I can't write another, I'm finished. I am broken."

I've written a number of other novels since then, so clearly that feeling was temporary and I now understand that the emptiness is just another part of the creative process.

So don't worry. This is normal. It happens to most writers after the end of a book. You have given your all to the manuscript and it has ripped you apart and taken everything, so it's natural to be empty.

Antidote:

Fill the creative well, then trust emergence. Something will come out of the milieu of this crazy, buzzing world and if you wait a little for the book to pass on, then ideas will start to emerge again and your mind will soon be filled with words waiting to be written. See the next chapter 1.9 if you're really struggling around ideas, and there's more in Part 3 on sorting out your creative process and managing the author journey.

Whatever the underlying problem, you won't overcome writer's block by moaning about it with author friends for weeks on Facebook … or by any other distraction mechanism. The only way to overcome it is through taking action to fix the underlying issue … and get back to writing.

"I deal with writer's block by lowering my expectations. I think the trouble starts when you sit down to write and imagine that you will achieve something magical and magnificent—and when you don't, panic sets in. The solution is never to sit down and imagine that you will achieve something magical and magnificent. I write a little bit, almost every day, and if it results in two or three or (on a good day) four good paragraphs, I consider myself a lucky man. Never try to be the hare. All hail the tortoise."

Malcolm Gladwell

1.9 "I'm not creative. I don't have any ideas."

"Every child is an artist. The problem is how to remain an artist once we grow up."

Pablo Picasso

I struggled with this for many years, truly believing that I was not a creative person.

"My family is very creative," I would tell people. "My Dad's a printmaker, my Mum paints, my sister is a textiles designer and my brother's a fashion designer. But I'm just not gifted in that way."

I've always loved books and learning and I did well in exams, so I went down an academic route, giving up art for ancient Greek (!!), and taking English Literature so very seriously so that I became stunted by what *should* be written, rather than even considering that I could write what I loved to read. As Sir Ken Robinson said in his fantastic TED talk, "We are educating people out of their creativity." That certainly happened to me.

I went to Oxford University, which made me even more serious about my studies, and emerged with a Masters in Theology, which led somehow to a career in consulting. Through a series of events that I didn't seem to actively choose, I ended up working in large corporates for 13 years, specializing in implementing financial systems into Accounts Payable departments. Can you imagine anything LESS creative than that?

I certainly don't regret my business career, as the skills I learned are valuable now as I run my own creative business, but I was miserable inside for many years, wondering why I didn't enjoy my work and why I felt so empty.

Then I started writing my first book and my life changed.

Ten years later, I make a full-time living with my writing and my company is called The Creative Penn. I decided to 'own' the word that I had rejected for so long.

So if you're someone who feels that they're 'just not creative,' what can you do about it?

Antidote:

Change your mindset

I knew I wanted to become more creative, but initially I didn't really know how to make a change in my life. I started to read self-help books and write notes in copious Moleskine journals. I listened to a lot of podcasts as well as buying audiobooks and programs to help me shift my mindset.

We cannot learn everything at once, and often I would listen to a whole audio program on my long commute and maybe only grasp one thing. But then I would listen again and another penny would drop. Over time, my knowledge about creativity grew. Listening to interviews can be inspiring because it helps you see that other people have made this shift, too. No one becomes successful on day one and we all start with nothing. This is partly why I started The

Creative Penn podcast, because I wanted to help others on the journey too.

One particular book changed my life. *The Success Principles* by Jack Canfield kicked my ass and made me take responsibility for my life and my choices over the years. It helped me decide what I really wanted and encouraged me to started saying an affirmation, "I am creative, I am an author," even though at that point in 2006 I didn't feel creative and I certainly wasn't an author!

It seems incredible now but I couldn't even say those words out loud at first. Maybe because they meant so much. I just wrote them in my journal and on a card I kept in my wallet. But over time, I began to whisper them on my walk home from the day job. Saying the words out loud articulated what I wanted to be, but also helped me gain confidence that I could achieve my goal. It took about 18 months from that affirmation to my first non-fiction book making it out into the world. A year after that, I started my website, TheCreativePenn.com and three years later, I left my day job to make a full-time living from my writing. That transition all began with a mindset shift.

"Creativity is not a talent. It's a way of operating."

John Cleese

Follow, and trust, your curiosity

Don't write what you know, write what you're interested in, and you will never run out of ideas. If you have a curious mind, then you will always be learning, always be experiencing and then you can use that as the basis for your books. If I want to learn about something new, I generally write a book about it, because I work out what I think while I'm writing. It clarifies and codifies the world into black and white and in the process of creating, I discover something new about myself. This is why much of my fiction has an edge of the supernatural and even the divine, because I'm still working out what I believe in. And my non-fiction is written based on what I need at the time, e.g. I wrote *Business for Authors: How to be an Author Entrepreneur* when I wanted to understand the way a creative business works and help others through the process.

Trusting your curiosity is also important. Before the Internet, it might have been hard to find other fans of the weird things that fascinate us, but now, you can always find others like you online. For example, I've always liked graveyards (I'm a taphophile) and it's likely that one in three people reading this also feel the same way. The others think we're weird! But that's OK. I never used to admit this in public because I was worried that people might think I'm strange, but once I did talk about it, I discovered a whole new community.

Now when I share photos on Pinterest of graveyards I visit on my travels, or beautiful sculptures or architecture that I find fascinating, those pictures resonate with others with the same interests, and when I put them into my books, they find the right audience.

Fill the creative well

You can't create from nothing. You can't sit down and expect to write without putting stuff into your brain first. You need material inside you to create from and that material has to come from somewhere. When I started, I had no ideas at all. I didn't know what to create, let alone how. Then I started going on what Julia Cameron described as 'the artist's date,' and that made all the difference.

Basically, you set aside some time to do something for your creative self. That might be going to an art gallery, or joining a creative class, or walking somewhere inspirational, or just reading for pleasure and not feeling guilty about all the other things you might be doing instead.

Then, while on your artist's date, start to notice your thoughts and questions, and importantly, write them down. I still use Moleskine journals but I also use the Things app on my iPhone where I have a folder for ideas. Others use Evernote. I write down anything that comes to mind, often one-liners, or even just one word.

Here are some of my recent notes:

- Ancient Chinese potters would write words in the mud before they made the mud into pots

- Bones don't bleed

- Secret patisserie chefs working in restaurants for people you will never hear of, in rooms you will never enter

- Monarch butterflies are called lost children as they arrive for Mexican Day of the Dead

- "Born into a myth called Prague" Kafka

I have many thousands of these little notes now. I scroll through them if I am considering a book idea, or just for fun. I often find that I've used the ideas in my writing without consciously finding them again. The brain is a marvelous thing indeed! Of course, if any of the ideas above spark something in you, please feel free to use them. Ideas are nothing, execution is everything!

Balance consumption with creation

Then, you need to take what you put into your brain and turn it into something else. This is the balance between consumption and creation, which needs to be kept in equilibrium.

If you consume too much, you won't have time to create. (If you're struggling to find time to write, count the hours you spend watching TV!)

If you create too much without filling your creative well, you may end up burned out because you're empty.

Start small and learn along the way

It's pretty much impossible to go from not feeling creative at all to tackling your first novel in a month. You're likely to fail and that can set you back a long time through discouragement. This happened to me many years ago when I gave up my job and cleared three months in my schedule to write a novel. I didn't have a clue what I was doing and just sat at my desk wondering why I was failing so badly. I ended up going back to the day job early. Years later when I tried again I spent a lot of time learning and started writing non-fiction first, as it has a shorter learning curve than fiction. I also kept my day job and wrote in my spare time, so there was no time or income pressure.

Learn to play

Stop being so serious about your writing. Be more like a child in your attitude toward creation. Enjoy the process. Maybe even smile or laugh sometimes, rather than furrowing your brow at the screen all the time. Sure, you need to get the book done and whatever's in your heart onto the page, but is it really so important?

Start before you know what you're doing

At some point, you have to stop reading books about creativity and writing, and actually create something and write! Of course, it's much safer just to keep learning but that won't help you reach your goal. You'll never know everything and you'll never exhaust the number of books or classes out there. So get started and learn on the journey. It's what the rest of us are doing!

> "You get ideas from daydreaming. You get ideas from being bored. You get ideas all the time. The only difference between writers and other people is we notice when we're doing it."
>
> *Neil Gaiman*

1.10 "My writing isn't original"

"Everybody is original, if he tells the truth, if he speaks from himself. But it must be from his true self and not from the self he thinks he should be."

Brenda Ueland

Every story has been written before.

Every non-fiction gem of wisdom has been said before.

All human experience has already been cataloged in countless books.

These truths can paralyze us, especially in the early days of writing when we don't know how to deal with the demons of self-doubt.

But *your* thoughts have not been written before, and *your* story has not been told before.

You are the original aspect of creativity, and what you bring to the world will be different to what others bring, even on the same topic.

Originality is just a twist on what has already gone before. As Picasso said, "Great artists steal." I read a lot of books on writing novels before I wrote a novel. I also read thousands of thrillers. But the penny dropped on how to actually write a novel when I deconstructed one in detail. I used *The Doomsday Key* by James Rollins, one of my favorite authors, and I broke down each chapter into what happened, point of view, length of chapter, first and last lines to look at cliffhangers, and much more. This kind of intense reading and deconstruction can be used to help you understand the structure of successful books, and you can do it for any genre, including non-fiction and memoir. You can then use that structure and what you've learned to put your own spin on the genre.

This is not plagiarism, which is directly copying people's work. It also doesn't mean taking another author's structure and directly reproducing it, changing names and places but keeping the same ideas. It's more about modeling and understanding what is working with specific books, noticing what keeps you enthralled as a reader and then using that process in your own work.

For example, I binge-read Jonathan Maberry's awesome *Joe Ledger* series recently and identified what I particularly liked about the books:

- Features a secret government agency tackling global conspiracies and a team of fighters, including strong female characters, led by a damaged assassin

- Techno-thriller elements of genetics and science

- Combined with a classical element of monsters and horror villains like vampires, zombies and mythical creatures

- Fast action pacing and high body count

I enjoy similar aspects in novels from James Rollins, Jeremy Robinson, Matthew Reilly and others, and I also weave them into my own thrillers.

Does that mean our books are all the same?

Not at all.

It means they will satisfy readers of this type of book and we all bring our original spin to the structure of an action-adventure thriller. In the same way, there are millions of books for writers out there, but this book is my experience shared in a way I hope will be useful for you.

Whatever you want to write, you need to be aware of the expectations of readers and what has gone before in order to take it into the realm of something new and put your own spin on the idea.

Antidote:

Embrace what has already been done and read a great deal in the genres you enjoy and want to write in. Elements from those books will resonate in your writing quite naturally, but you can then take them further by bringing in your imagination and your voice.

Don't obsess over perceived imitation or cliché in a first draft. Just get the words down and as you self-edit, go through and fix it up.

"Those who do not want to imitate anything,
produce nothing."

Salvador Dali

1.11 "Why write? There are already too many books in the world"

"Why write? Why breathe?"

Katherine Mansfield

A child comes to you with a new drawing, crayon in hand, beaming with pleasure at creation and proud of the result. Do you say, "There are too many drawings in the world and this is no good. Stop creating immediately."

Or do you say, "That's brilliant. Why don't you draw another one?"

Your creative self is that child. When you start to constrain what is possible to create, that child will cower in fear and stop creating.

Some in the industry say that there are too many books in the world.

That you are competing for a small pool of readers.

That you shouldn't help your fellow authors because they might get ahead of you.

I shall use the term 'poppycock' since we are in polite company and I'm British, but there are other less polite words you could apply to these thoughts.

If you believe that there can only be a specific number of

books in the world i.e. those that are judged worthy by a few privileged gatekeepers, then you are crushing the voices of unheard people in every culture, as well as your own creativity.

I bet you were a reader before you were a writer, as was I. Perhaps your parents read to you at night when you were little. Maybe you read under the bedclothes as you got older. Maybe your idea of fun was sneaking off to the library every lunchtime. Perhaps books are your hobby, your passion and your escape – as they are for me.

I don't know how many books I've read in my 41 years of life so far, but I can tell you, it is many thousands more than I have written, and many more than I will ever be able to write in my lifetime. The most prolific authors, like Nora Roberts, write as many as twelve books per year, but you can bet they still read more than one a month. One author alone can never satisfy a reader's appetite.

Antidote:

Writers are readers first.

Understand that every person who writes a book, or wants to write one, will end up buying far more books than they can ever create themselves. If everyone in the world wrote a book, fantastic! All of them will read many more than they write. So encourage all your friends and family to write immediately.

Cultivate an abundance mentality and you will be far happier. Find authors in your niche who serve the same audience as you. Read their books and recommend them to your readers. Give without expectation of receiving. More on this in Part 3.4.

1.12 "I don't have the time or self-discipline to write"

"Forcing yourself to write is like forcing yourself to run. Once you get into it, you love it, and you wonder why you resisted."

Natalie Goldberg

Writing is simple but it's not easy. Getting black on white can sometimes seem like the hardest thing in the world to achieve, and yet we are nothing without words on a page. Getting them down takes time, and setting the time aside usually takes discipline at first, until we develop a creative habit. Even then, there are tough days. Here's an excerpt from my journal in 2014:

"Today has been a difficult day. I procrastinated when I should have been writing. I emailed instead of creating things. I did busywork and admin that didn't achieve much. I spent time on Twitter instead of writing. I bet Stephen King wouldn't behave like this. He would sit at his desk and write something new. Today I am a tired, disillusioned misery. But tomorrow I will be an author again. I promise."

We will always have times like these, and the challenge to find time is a daily struggle. There are also increasing demands on a writer's time. Should you attend this summit or do this online course? Should you build your author platform and start blogging or podcasting? Should you spend time on social media building relationships and finding readers even before your book is done?

There are pros and cons with all of these ways to spend time, but ultimately, writers write, they don't just talk (or tweet or blog or Facebook or Instagram) about writing.

If you don't make the time to write the words for your books, you are the only one who suffers, as I did in the journal excerpt above. If you keep avoiding making the time to write, you will feel like a failure. You'll wonder what you're doing with your life. You'll be disappointed at your lack of progress. The only person who will beat you up about your writing is yourself, and you are the only one who can make the time.

Antidote:

I'm pretty sure you know what you have to do, but here are my tips:

How much do you really want this?

Everyone has the same amount of time and you can usually tell what people value by how they spend it. Of course, you have to balance a day job and family commitments, but if you have a free hour, what do you do with it?

My own turning point came when I really committed to the writing path. I never really enjoyed my consulting job, but I stuck it out for many years, thinking that it was just what I had to do to get by. It was only when I was crying at work and wondering what the hell I was doing with my life, that my motivation became large enough to overcome my excuses. Instead of staying in bed in the morning, I got up at 5am to write, learn and build my platform. When I got home after work, I didn't watch TV, but read books on writing, creative business and online marketing. At the weekends, I ducked out of social arrangements in order to have a whole day to work on my writing. Then I told my boss I only wanted to work four days a week and negotiated a 20% reduction in hours and income so I could have that extra day. Three years later, I left my day job because I had built a sustainable creative business.

But only because I really wanted it and I made the time.

So how much do you want it?

Diarize your writing time

Book an appointment with yourself, as you would with a business or personal meeting. Don't just think, "Oh, I'll find 20 mins sometime today." Get your planner out and schedule 20 mins or an hour, or whatever you can, at a specific time. Set a timer if necessary. If you're a parent, I bet you schedule your kid's activities. And for your day job, I bet you schedule appointments at specific times. You certainly schedule social engagements and you probably even schedule the gym. So why not take your writing just as seriously?

When you're in front of the page or keyboard, stay there. Setting a goal around word count or a deadline in terms of time completed can help. Don't get up until you have something to show for your time. That may be structure or story ideas or research notes or first draft writing, but get something down. Until you get into the practice of producing words on the page, you will struggle.

To get those ideas down, you have to just give it a go and write words. What happens next? What do I want to say? Just write something and edit it later.

"What people say they want and what they're willing to work their ass off to get are two different things."

Hugh MacLeod

1.13 "I'm not finding writing much fun. It's hard work."

"I hate writing. I love having written."

Dorothy Parker

The writer's life has traditionally been shrouded in myth, and the truth of the hard work involved has been discreetly veiled by the publishing industry and by authors themselves. This means that many new writers think that all one has to do is sit down and start typing and miraculously the Muse will alight and bestow a blessing and the book will stream out in perfect sentences. Thus a prize-winning and bestselling book is born and the author is destined for super-stardom.

But I don't think that has ever been the truth.

Organizing ideas and plotting and outlining is hard, writing first draft words is difficult and editing can be the most painful part as you try to wrestle your manuscript into something others might want to read. By the end of the process, you are likely to be seriously over this book and you will never want to read it again!

Here's an excerpt from my journal in 2010:

"It's so hard writing a book. I feel like I'm wading through mud up to my waist in a rain storm. Every step is an effort. The weight drags me backward, sucking me down. Then I get a clear patch and the sun comes out and I surprise myself with what I write, and it's actually alright. Then

the mud sucks and I am bogged down again. Does this ever get better?"

Here's an excerpt from an email I received from a fellow writer:

"Literally every single person I've ever met thinks they could also be a writer. The popular image of a writer is that we put on a funny hat, slug back some whiskey, and pound out an award-winning manuscript in one long night. That mythology has zero regard for the planning, outlining, plotting, editing, rewriting, editing again – the ages and ages and ages of WORK. Sometimes I roll my eyes at those people. But most of the time it is so draining. They really, genuinely think my job is that easy! I can't think of any other creative pursuit that everyone else is so completely convinced they could do if only they had a few free hours."

And here's a quote from multi-award-winning author Haruki Murakami: "For me writing a novel is like climbing a steep mountain, struggling up the face of the cliff, reaching the summit after a long and arduous ordeal."

And more from Ernest Hemingway, "There is nothing to writing. All you do is sit down at a typewriter and bleed."

And finally, George Orwell, author of literary classics *1984* and *Animal Farm*: "Writing a book is a horrible, exhausting struggle, like a long bout of some painful illness. One would never undertake such a thing if one were not driven on by some demon whom one can neither resist nor understand."

Clearly, writing a book is not an easy task for many of the greatest writers, so why expect it to be for you?

Antidote:

Decide why you want to write and that will pull you through the difficult parts

I love the research process, the weave of ideas, the rush of discovery and the feeling of satisfaction that comes from creating a new book in the world. I sometimes wonder where the words come from, and that little mystery is like an inner secret that makes life exciting. I also like to help and inspire people through my non-fiction. I write because I want some kind of immortality, because otherwise I'll have nothing to show for the years that pass. I measure my life by what I create, and every day, I'm grateful that I am not stuck in my old corporate consulting day job. I also have a craving to write if I go too long without the blank page. I get grumpy when I don't write. It's my therapy, my indulgence, but also my truth, my craft, the way I think, my only way of processing the world.

These reasons carry me through the hard parts. So why do you write? What will carry you through the difficult times?

It doesn't have to be so hard. Enjoy it if you can!

Then there's the truly radical thought that writing doesn't actually have to be that hard. It can even be fun and enjoyable! As veteran author of several hundred novels, Dean Wesley Smith, says, "You need to let the two year old play."

My two year old inner creative was shut down for years, through exams and rigorous testing, through being a good girl at school, college and then getting a 'proper' corporate job. My husband says that I'm a serious little sausage and play is anathema to my Protestant work ethic. But I've been trying to unlearn much of this.

I've started doing coloring before writing, as my inner creative child likes color and stickers and lovely stationery. I even published an adult coloring book with my Dad! I'm trying to laugh more as I create and write down the silly things that come, without censoring them. Maybe you could also try having fun with your writing?

"You do not need to save the world. Your art doesn't need to be important … It's okay if your work is fun for you, or healing or fascinating or frivolous. It's all allowed. Your own reasons to create are enough … Enjoying your work with all your heart is the only truly subversive position left to take!"

Elizabeth Gilbert, Big Magic

1.14 "I keep starting things and not finishing them"

"The road to hell is paved with works-in-progress."

Philip Roth

I was speaking in central London and a fantasy author friend of mine arrived early to have a chat over coffee.

"How's your writing going?" I asked.

He grinned and his blue eyes lit up. "Awesome! I have 15 different projects and I'm writing 4,000 words a day. I've just got so many ideas."

"Wow!" I replied. "Sales must be great with 15 books out there."

His smile fell, his eyes dimmed.

"Oh, they're not published, or edited … or even finished. I've got 15 different books in first draft. I love writing new words but I'm just not interested in the rest of the process."

Do you have unfinished books in the drawer or on your laptop?

Do you start with a few pages and then move onto something new?

Do you lose interest in the project once the initial excitement wears off?

Antidote:

If you want to be a successful author, you have to develop the skills you are lacking. Writing a book has several phases, each associated with different types of energy.

Starting energy

Once you start paying attention to your creative side, ideas will never be a problem again. The problem will be deciding which ideas to pursue and turn into a book. Once you have decided, those first few thousand words can be an adrenaline rush. The opening scenes come easily and the structure of a book appears quickly. If you feel this way, you have starting energy and it will carry you through to perhaps 20,000 words of a full-length manuscript. (If you're writing a novella, congratulations, you're almost done!)

But if you struggle with starting, then there are a couple of things to consider:

- Don't try to write the first chapter or the first scene or the introduction first. That can come later. Try starting in the middle, or with a piece of writing you are particularly passionate about instead. Just start and fill in the rest later.

- Are you procrastinating because of fear?

- Are you being perfectionist and waiting for some kind of perfect idea or perfect situation before writing?

- Are you suffering from paralysis by analysis? I recognize this, as I spent years reading books on writing and going to seminars without doing much actual writing. Just get some words on the page!

Pushing through energy

This is the one I struggle with (along with many authors) and is known as the 'saggy middle.' For a novel, I generally know my opening scene, climactic scene and a couple of big scenes throughout and then I start writing. By about 25,000 words of a full-length novel, I find myself stuck and losing focus. I start to struggle. This is a common issue and the same happens with non-fiction. Writers who outline don't suffer this so much, but instead they may find themselves bored by having to write what they've already outlined and thus revisiting the same material.

The only resolution is to set specific word count goals and keep writing. This is not a 'how to write' book so I won't go into the details here but you can find more on writing here: www.TheCreativePenn.com/writing

Finishing energy

If you struggle to finish anything, then don't start a new book before you've finished the one you're working on, especially if you are just starting out. It's that simple!

I'll add a caveat to that. You can have one fiction and one non-fiction first draft in progress, since I believe they use different parts of the brain. But from my own personal experience, it's difficult to work on two novels at the same time or even two non-fiction books. I start to confuse them and it all goes a little nuts. Sure, during the writing of one book, I'll be thinking about other story ideas and I add notes in my Things app, but I won't write coherent words on a new project until I am done with the one I'm working on, or at least when it's gone to my editor.

"You must finish what you start."

Robert A. Heinlein, from Heinlein's Rules

1.15 Dealing with family, friends and writers' groups

"Why can't you write something nice?"

"Why don't you write something more like [insert famous writer name here] and then you might be more successful?"

"I've got a great idea, maybe you can write about it and we'll split the money."

"I like this chapter but your main character is just so wrong."

"Maybe you should just rewrite the whole thing."

"Why are you even bothering to write? It's a waste of time."

Have you heard these words or something like them from your family, friends or writers' group? How did that make you feel? Is this really useful feedback?

When you start out writing, your inner creative is just a little seedling with tiny leaves above the earth, peeping out into the air for the first time. It's very easy for that seedling to be crushed into the ground by harsh words or judgment that leave it bruised and battered and unable to rise again. You have to care for it, protect and nurture it until it becomes a little stronger. Then the wind and rain can come and it will bend but not be crushed. It will even become stronger as it resists the push of the weather, but still, it will be vulnerable. You need to care for your creative self as you would any fragile new life.

Our family and friends may love us but they are unlikely to understand our need to write, unless they are creatives themselves. The range of responses to the writing life range from enthusiastic support of our endeavors, through disinterest and uncaring, all the way to shaming, or even verbal abuse. Try not to take it personally. It may be a reaction to an unfulfilled creative longing within them, or just not understanding why this is important to you. It's tough, but generally our family and friends are *not* our potential readers.

Then there are writers' groups. If you're in one already and it's full of published authors in your genre who are supportive, sensitive and generous with their feedback, then great. But in my experience, most writers' groups do more harm than good and I frequently get emails from people who feel attacked in them. These groups are generally full of unpublished writers who may not even read the genre you're writing in. They pull apart each other's work and a new writer faced with a load of untargeted feedback from too many other people is likely to lose their way in the process.

Antidote:

Accept that your family and friends may not be the best people to support your writer's journey. They may never read your book, and if they do, they might not like it anyway. This is hard to hear but it's best to be prepared.

Examine the groups you're in and the friendships you have around writing. Are they helping that fragile seedling to flourish? Or are they stomping on your growth?

It might be better to pay a professional editor within your genre to critique and improve your work, and join an informal writers' group for social interaction and support, not for critical feedback on your writing.

I have an almost entirely different friendship group now than I did back in my corporate consulting days. I've changed, my life has changed and I have little in common with the friends I once hung out with. You have to clear space for something new to emerge and it may be hard, but sometimes, you have to do that if you want to grow. See chapter 3.6 for ways to find your new community as a writer.

"Poisonous people do not deserve your time."

Timothy Ferriss

1.16 "How do I find my voice?"

> "I write only because there is a voice within me
> that will not be still."
>
> *Sylvia Plath*

Finding your voice is not a quick process! For me, it was only after years of blogging and several books that I started to find mine, and it's something that continues to evolve over time.

What is your 'voice' anyway?

It's essentially a way of communicating the authentic you and happens when you embrace what you love without being embarrassed or self-censoring, knowing that there are others out there like you who will resonate with it. It emerges when you stop writing things just because you think other people will like them and when you stop apologizing for what you write.

When you stop trying to be like the writers you admire and begin to emerge as yourself.

When you stop writing the same thing that others are writing.

When you share what you love with pride.

When you accept that you will turn people off as well as attracting people who love what you do.

It's the real you, with no protective screen in front.

And that's hard to get to.

You should be able to hear my voice in this book and if you listen to my podcast, you shouldn't notice any difference, because my non-fiction is written with my authentic, real-life voice. If you read a number of my novels, you'll hear my fiction voice, my shadow side, which is different but still distinctive.

We all have different facets that we share with the world. I behave differently at home with my husband than I do when speaking to an audience at an event. I'm different with my Mum than I am with a close friend. I'm different when I'm in introvert writing silent mode, to when I'm having a few drinks with my author mates at a convention. But my inner voice and my essential self remain the same, it's a core within me that you will either resonate with or not.

And you have to find what that is for you, too.

Finding your voice is about knowing yourself, and letting yourself be the writer you really are. Here are some questions that might help:

- What fascinates you?

- What are the themes that you keep returning to in your work? What obsesses you?

- What images, colors and photos are you drawn to?

- What do you like to read or watch or listen to? What are your favorite books or films or songs? What do they have in common?

- What makes you angry or sad, happy or aroused? What stirs your emotions?

- What do you stand for? What do you defend?

Answer these truthfully, without judgment, without considering what the answer 'should' be.

Writers find their voice through writing, and for me and many others, it takes a number of books before you really get into your stride. Writing *Desecration* was the turning point for me as someone fascinated by demons and the supernatural, as someone who ponders the deeper side of life and writes death in every story. Despite trying to write 'straight' thrillers, everything I wrote had a supernatural edge. So now I lean into my crazy and embrace what my true self wants to write about.

Earlier chapters cover self-censorship and fear, but here are a few more tips for finding your voice.

Use journaling or free writing

Not every word you write has to be shared with the public! Writing your own truth takes practice and sometimes it's best NOT to be sharing that stuff! Write freely and experiment, write terrible poetry or rant about whatever you like. Read your words back with acceptance or just put them in a drawer. Check out Orna Ross' books on free writing for more on this at www.OrnaRoss.com

Use blogging or Wattpad

Blogging changed my life. Before 2008, my writing consisted of over a decade of academic and business writing, stilted, concise corporate speak which curbed any personality. Blogging released my inhibited style and allowed my personality to come through. I've written over 1,000 blog posts on TheCreativePenn.com in the last eight years. That's a lotta words, and the practice of writing in public and feedback through social media and comments has released my inhibitions about sharing what's in my mind.

If you'd rather not blog, you could try Wattpad.com, an online writing and reading platform where people post their stories in progress, while they are still in creation mode. The style is relaxed and there's a lot of fan fiction. It can certainly be a way to build an audience for your work, but because of its relaxed format, it can also be a way to lean into your voice.

Essentially, however you look at it, you find your voice through writing. Of course, it will develop and change over time. Like the layers of your personality, you'll find new depths to your voice and your expression.

"Every secret of a writer's soul, every experience of his life, every quality of his mind, is written large in his works."

Virginia Woolf

1.17 Comparisonitis or "Everyone else is better than me"

"The amateur continuously rates himself in relation to others, becoming self-inflated if his fortunes rise, and desperately anxious if his star should fall. The amateur craves third-party validation."

Steven Pressfield, Turning Pro

OUCH.

That hurts because I know I get comparisonitis sometimes. It's hard not to when you hear about the latest seven-figure book deal or read about an indie author hitting the best-seller lists or selling their film rights.

Even if you're writing your first book as part of a local group or a college course, there will always be people you compare yourself to and you may find yourself wanting.

I was at the London Book Fair recently where agents sit in endless meetings trying to sell books to publishers across the world, and every day they announce exciting deals coming out of the Rights Center. They also have billboard-size photos of name brand authors, the A-list movie stars of the book world. Walking beneath them, I felt like the smallest, most inadequate writer on the planet. It felt like every author in the world was doing better than I was, and yes, I was jealous of that success.

Because that's the dark side of comparing yourself to others. It can morph into jealousy, and that can turn toxic. It must be dealt with or it will eat you up inside.

"Resentment is like drinking poison and hoping it will kill your enemies."

Nelson Mandela

Antidote:

Start by realizing that you can only compare yourself to who *you* were as a writer last year. We are all at different points on the writer's journey and we only ever hear the highlights in the media. We don't know what happened to that suddenly-famous debut author before their breakout book and we might be mistakenly comparing ourselves to someone who has been ghostwriting under another name for ten years, or have five novels that were rejected before the one that hit big.

This is why I like blogging, as I can look back at where I was over the years and track the change – in my writing craft, my income and book sales, my platform and my knowledge. Even if you just journal once a year, it's worth doing to track changes over time and turn comparisonitis into a positive way for you to measure progress.

If you feel the pull of comparisonitis or even jealousy, recognize that feeling and be aware of it. If you know how you feel, you can control your behavior. I've seen some authors damage their reputations by attacking others' success and it's ugly. One author wrote an article calling for J.K.

Rowling to stop writing because she'd had her success and it was time to let others have a turn.

But first of all, Rowling is a writer. She *will* write and as a fan of her later Robert Galbraith books, I'm glad she continues to do so.

Secondly, this is a poverty mindset, the thought that there are only a certain number of readers or amount of money in the world and that one author's success takes away our own potential future.

But that's not true.

So let's try to reframe comparisonitis and the edge of jealousy into something that can actually help us become better writers.

If you find someone who triggers that feeling, research that author's background. Read their book/s. How long have they been writing? What did they do to get to where they are? How can you emulate them and use their example to further your own craft and author career?

You could even turn what you learn into a blog post or journal entry or add items to your To Do list. If I read a book by an author I have been jealous of and I like it, I'll always promote it to my own audience in the ultimate reversal of jealousy. Celebrate the success of other authors and it will make you a happier writer, plus it will build your network over time.

"Stop looking at what other people are doing and look at what you're achieving. Stop looking sideways, look at where you're going."

Jocelyn Glei, Manage your Day to Day

Part 2: Mindset Aspects after Publishing

2.1 Anti-climax and creative dissatisfaction

[Don't read this chapter if you haven't published yet!]

"The moment of completion is also, inevitably, a moment of loss."

David Bayles & Ted Orland, Art and Fear

At some point, the book is done and out in the world. You have overcome all the issues of creation and publication and now the book is finished. You've done the best you could with that idea … so why do you feel a sense of anti-climax?

It might be disappointment with sales. You've spent months planning the launch of your book, either with your publisher or on your own as an indie. You've booked blog tours and made friends on social media. Maybe you've got a book trailer done and your website is ready. You've done everything people say you should do.

Then, yippee! Your book is launched to the world and on the first day, it sells 200 copies.

Not 20,000 or even 2,000.

Just 200.

Over the next month, it sells a few hundred more, but it has not set the world on fire and you are not rolling in cash.

You're crushed. You're embarrassed when people ask you about it in the coffee shop or in that private Facebook group.

You're questioning everything.

It might also be creative dissatisfaction, the feeling that however hard you tried with the book, you have more to say, more to give, more to write.

Sure, you've had some bubbles to celebrate, but you're feeling a little flat.

You've been driving hard toward this goal for so long, and now you've reached it, the experience just doesn't quite match your expectations.

This is one of the surprising things as a writer, because the myth of publishing is that launch day is some kind of magical occasion when all your dreams come true.

But it rarely is.

The reality of publication doesn't live up to the dream.

In fact, the most disappointed authors I've met are those whose first book has just come out, because they've realized that the work has just started. The next time around, most authors are more realistic about what happens and those who continue truly can't see themselves doing anything else.

Antidote:

One of the inherent parts of being human is a general dissatisfaction with where we are, even if we try to be grateful in the moment. However much we achieve, we often want more. This has an evolutionary benefit, as it means we are always striving, always creating, always building.

I've come to understand that this particular dissatisfaction is just part of the creative process, and publication is not actually meant to be the high point. The real joy is more often felt during the creation process itself, when you come up with some awesome idea, or when you finish a satisfying chapter. That's when I break out the gin and tonic and feel that sense of accomplishment and pride.

Sure, I love to hold my finished book in my hand and say, "I made this!" but once the book is done, I'm ready to move onto the next one. I've also found that this feeling gets even more pronounced as the number of books stack up.

When people write their first or second book, they talk about books as children, but when you're up to book fifteen or fifty, you tend to just finish it and move on. Yes, you should celebrate your successes, and that first book in particular is a big one, since most people never even finish a book. But if your intention is to write as a career, then a new book is just another waypoint on the journey, a link in the chain, another aspect of your body of work.

Disappointment is also a necessary experience, because it is this feeling that drives us to the next project and makes the creative process so addictive. Because we will always be learning and changing along the journey.

There will never be perfection, because if there was, we

would stop creating. That's why I love this life. Writing is a career you can do until the day you die, because you can never exhaust the depth and breadth of your mind or your curiosity.

"I still encourage anyone who feels at all compelled to write to do so. I just try to warn people who hope to get published that publication is not all it is cracked up to be.

But writing is.

Writing has so much to give, so much to teach, so many surprises. That thing you had to force yourself to do – the actual act of writing – turns out to be the best part. It's like discovering that while you thought you needed the tea ceremony for the caffeine, what you really needed was the tea ceremony. The act of writing turns out to be its own reward."

Anne Lamott

2.2 What is your definition of success?

"Writing isn't about making money, getting famous, getting dates, getting laid, or making friends. In the end it's about enriching the lives of those who will read your work, and enriching your own life as well."

Stephen King

A lot of the dissatisfaction described in the last chapter comes from not being clear about your definition of success. Publishing a book for many people is a nebulous goal that has dollar signs and media mentions attached to it, but often hasn't been specified clearly enough. So whatever stage you're at on the writer's journey, identifying your definition of success will help a great deal.

Why are you writing?

Why do you want your book published and out in the world for others to read?

Go beyond the initial answer to the deeper reasons we create because writers are not a homogenous bunch, and we all strive for different things, for different reasons, and this may change over time. But it's important to identify these so you can measure your journey, celebrate your successes and understand how far you've come over time.

It comes down to three questions:

- What is your definition of success – for this particular book and for your writing career?

- How will you track and measure that success?

- What do you want to do with that success? What is the point in your creative work?

Your answers will also tend to change over time, as your definition of success will be dependent on the progression of your writing career. Here are some of the more common variations as well as potential options for measuring them. All of them are valid and possible. The important thing is to decide what you're aiming for.

(1) It's my life goal to write a book. I want to create something I'm proud of and hold my book in my hand

This is perhaps where we all start – with the desire to finish a project and create something tangible. This is also why most first-time authors want a printed book that they can put on the shelf and show people. The focus of success here is on a creative project, which is a totally brilliant reason to write! For example, I helped my nine-year-old niece publish her first book, which led to her winning a national prize for speaking publicly about the experience. I also helped my Dad with his historical thriller, *Nada*. Neither of these are commercial prospects, but success can be achieved through self-publishing a few copies for friends and family.

If this is your goal, check out www.TheCreativePenn.com/ publishing for your options and look at print-on-demand. If you don't want to do it yourself, I recommend that you read *Choosing a Self-Publishing Service* by the Alliance of Independent Authors so you can avoid the (ever-increasing) scams in this growing industry.

(2) I want to get an agent and a publishing deal

This is easy to measure in terms of whether you make this goal, but remember that every agent and every publisher has their own definition of success e.g. some want a celebrity memoir that will sell millions, others may publish poetry for the love of it with no consideration of financial return. Make sure that the agent/publisher's goals match what you want to achieve. Choose who you pitch to wisely. Then consider what other aspects of success are important to you, because publication is only one step on the journey.

(3) I want to see my book on the shelves of a bookstore

We have shopped in bookstores all our lives and for many of us, the bookstore is a place of solace as well as adventure. When I was most miserable in my old day job, I would go to the bookstore at lunchtime and indulge in retail therapy to escape my life for a time. To see a book with our own name on it on those shelves must surely be every author's dream.

If you get a traditional publishing deal that includes print publication (and many are digital-only these days), then you will get into some physical bookstores. But remember that bookshops can only carry a limited number of books for a limited amount of time, so most that are not perennial sellers remain for a month and then are returned to the publisher to make way for the next batch of releases.

If you self-publish, it is difficult to get into physical bookstores, although it is possible. It's costly even if you can manage it because of heavy discounting and returns. You can definitely achieve this through services like Ingram Spark, and it's also possible to build relationships with your local bookstore so they will stock your books.

(4) I want to reach readers with my words

It's great to focus on readers, but I always challenge this definition of success, because it is so intangible. If you want to reach readers, then just put your book out for free on every platform in the world. But generally most people don't mean this kind of 'reach.'

So be more specific with this type of definition. How can you measure it? For example, is it achieved when you have ten five-star star reviews on Amazon, or you receive a fan email from a reader you've never met? Or do you really want to measure success by book sales?

(5) I want to sell 10,000 books

This is a better definition than (4) because it is measurable and you will know when you get there. The number is obviously dependent on many things e.g. the genre you write in, as a children's picture book will sell far fewer copies than a commercial romance novel; a narrative non-fiction memoir will generally sell less than a commercial thriller. It is also dependent on how many books you have, as you will more easily reach higher sales figures with more books.

This volume type of definition will also change over time. I started off with 1,000 books as a goal when I only had one book. Then I moved to 10,000, and I've now sold over 400,000 books, so my goals have changed again to aim for 1 million books sold. You can make it more specific if you include a timeline e.g. I want to sell 1,000 books in the first six months of publication.

(6) I want to receive critical acclaim and win a literary prize

You're far more likely to win a literary prize if you go through the traditional publishing route. It's the goal of most Master of Fine Arts (MFA) or Creative Writing programs to produce books capable of winning prizes. As for critical acclaim, again, you're more likely to get that through traditional publishing and reviews in literary journals.

However, it is possible to achieve this as an independent author. *A Naked Singularity* by Sergio de la Pava started out as self-published and won the PEN/Robert W. Bingham prize and was shortlisted for the Folio prize. The Alliance of Independent Authors also has an Open Up To Indies campaign, which will hopefully mean that more prizes and festivals open up to self-published books over time.

If this is your goal, you should also be aware of research that shows literary prizes can make the book less popular and most literary novels will sell fewer than 5,000 copies. So this definition of success may be incompatible with financial goals and significant sales volume.

(7) I want to make a full-time living with my writing

The definition of 'full-time living' is different by country, even by region, as well as the huge difference between income needs for a family with kids to a professional couple or single writer, so be specific about the actual figure you're aiming for. Think about how that may grow over time based on how much you're writing over the next few years, as well as your own financial requirements.

Then have a look at AuthorEarnings.com to see if your genre is likely to earn that kind of money. I also go into a lot more detail about how to do this in my book, *How to Make a Living with your Writing*.

This became my definition of success in 2009 and was bound up with my self-esteem as a financially independent woman, as well as wanting to live life on my own terms. After much hard work, I left my job as a business consultant in September 2011 to become a full-time author entrepreneur, and I've never gone back to the day job, so it is possible!

Of course, an income goal is not necessary for everyone, and for many, creativity alone is the reward. The full-time writing life is not for everyone.

(8) I want to create a body of work that I am proud of over my lifetime

This is the definition that will keep you honest about your creative output. You won't rush a book to publication. You won't put a book out without a professional edit, or a professional cover. You will strive for the best this particular project can be.

In the end, I want to write for the rest of my life, hopefully for at least another 50 years, so I'm in this for the long haul. But the creative journey *is* the point and there is no final end game. I want to earn a good living, but more than that, I want to be able to keep creating until the day I am no longer able.

"You're entitled to your labor,
not the fruits of your labor."

Krishna, quoted by Steven Pressfield in Turning Pro

2.3 What happens when you tell people that you're an author?

I'm at a party, clutching my wine glass in the corner, waiting for the alcohol to warm up my introvert tendencies. A friend of a friend drifts over.

"So I hear you're a writer?" she says. "What do you write?"

"Thrillers," I reply. "And some non-fiction."

"Ooh, are you famous? Have I heard of you?"

"Hmm. It's unlikely, to be honest. There are only a few name brand authors that everyone's heard of, like J.K. Rowling or Stephen King."

"Oh, right." She takes a sip of her Pinot Grigio. "So can I find your book in the bookstore?"

"Yes, on the biggest online bookstores in the world actually. Amazon, iBooks, Kobo."

She frowns. "I meant the physical bookstore down the road."

"Well, no. Physical bookstores only have room for a limited number of books."

"So who's your publisher?"

"Authors can publish direct these days. I'm an independent creative, like an indie musician without a big label, or an indie film-maker."

"Right …" She frowns, clearly confused. "Actually, I've always wanted to write a novel," she says. "Maybe one day when I have the time." She leans closer, whispering conspiratorially. "I have a really good idea though. If I tell you, maybe you can write it and we can split the money?"

Most writers have an anecdote that goes something like this. For some reason, people think it's easy to write a book and that ideas are the most important thing, rather than the hard work of execution. The reading public also seem to think that all authors are rich and famous, that books will be available in every bookstore and that every author has the experience of being a brand name author.

This can make you feel like an underachiever whatever you say, because they are comparing you to the rich and famous, and you may end up feeling upset and resentful, worrying why you're not able to live up to the expectations of others.

Antidote:

Don't take it personally! Amazingly, we've all had these exact conversations, so once you start having them, you know you've joined the exclusive author club. This person is likely one of the millions who say they want to write a book, but never do. You have already achieved far more than they can realize, so smile in a knowing way and take another sip of your wine. Or maybe a gulp …

2.4 "I'm overwhelmed"

"There's a hell of a lot more to art than just making it."

David Bayles & Ted Orland, Art and Fear

Overwhelm is not confined to the life of an author, but it's certainly one of the most common problems. Nowadays an author has to:

- Learn the craft of writing and improve over time by continuing the learning process

- Write fantastic books, often multiple books per year

- Work on edits

- Coordinate cover design if self-publishing

- Build an author platform through blogging or podcasting or video or social media, or all of them

- Build an email list of readers and engage with them regularly

- Network with other authors and service providers as well as maintaining professional relationships

- Market the book through any and all means

- Go to live events and possibly even speak at them

- Manage the business side if you're successful

- Get on with writing the next book

- Oh yes, and all that 'real life' stuff …

Many authors say, "I just want to write, I don't want to do all the rest. I want someone else to do it for me." But there are always parts of any job, or even life in general, that you don't enjoy or that have to be done for practical reasons. Admin never goes away!

Antidote:

Decide what is really important and then say no to everything else

Write down everything that you feel you have to do and that is making you feel overwhelmed. Then revisit your definition of success from chapter 2.2. Strike out the things on your list that will not get you closer to what you really want.

I'll admit that I struggle with this, because I feel like I want to do so much, and let's face it, it's easier to blog or hang out on social media 'doing book marketing,' than it is to do the writing work. But when it comes down to it, the most important thing will always be the writing. Without it, everything else is pointless.

A useful book on focus is *The One Thing* by Gary Keller.

Get over fear of missing out

Much of the clutter in our lives comes from the fear of missing out. We check social media and blogs for the latest posts, we check email too often in case we miss something, we attend another online course or webinar in case this time there will be a silver bullet that can change everything. But the minutes tick away and we've added more to the list of overwhelm and things to do and the words have not been written for another day.

Yes, you will always miss out on something. Get over it. Life is happening on the page and in your mind, just as much as it is out there.

Consider how you usually manage competing priorities

Life is a series of constant adjustments and being an author is no different. The see-saw may be balanced for a short amount of time and then it tips one way or the other. I'm not going to list a ton of productivity tips because somehow you are managing to get things done in the rest of your life, so you must learn how to manage your writing life in the same way.

"Anyone who dreams of an uncommon life eventually discovers there is no choice but to seek an uncommon approach to living it."

Gary Keller, The One Thing

2.5 Dealing with fans. Authenticity and drawing the line

"Ultimately the product that any writer has to sell is not the subject being written about, but who he or she is."

William Zinsser

I recently had coffee with a writer friend of mine whose first book had hit the Amazon UK number 1 spot. Of course, she was thrilled with her success but also surprised at what happened next.

"I had visions of a quiet life writing books," she said. "But suddenly I'm getting tons of email from fans and requests for interviews and it's just crazy."

It's fantastic to have such success, but every level of the author journey has its own challenges, and once people know who you are, they will start asking something of you. They may email with questions, they might contact you on social media, and you will eventually get asked to speak. You won't be able to hide away forever. This may be difficult at first and you'll have to work out how to deal with this type of interaction.

If this happens, congratulations! People actually care about your book, and this is fantastic and doesn't happen for everyone. But many writers seem to resent this kind of attention, even though it is the norm in a digital age. The writer cannot be alone in the garret anymore!

Of course, writers have always had to deal with the public and media opportunities. In the past, they replied to letters, whereas now you write emails, go on podcast interviews from your living room, and chat on Facebook.

Antidote:

If people love your book, they will want to meet you, read more words from you, hear your story in person or online through a website or social media. Readers want to connect with authors. They enjoyed the genuine human experience and emotion in your writing, so naturally they want to take it further. If you choose to publish and put your words into the world, then you have basically asked for a human response, so get used to it!

You are also interesting, even if you don't believe it. You are an author and that's a special thing for many people. Even the place where you write and the flowers in your garden, or the exploits of your cat, will be interesting to people on the other side of the world.

Putting yourself out there may make you feel vulnerable, but authenticity is what connects people. It's even possible to be authentic with a pseudonym, as you can still be you even if you use another name, but if you fake an entire persona, then it will eventually be uncovered. The only defense is to be yourself and the great thing about the Internet is that you will find people like you, whatever you're interested in. I always get the most comments, tweets and enthusiastic response when I'm at my most honest.

Because real life resonates.

Of course, you do need to curate yourself. Being authentic doesn't mean sharing everything about your life. It means sharing what you think is appropriate for the audience you want to connect to. For example, I don't share about my latest attempts with weight loss on Twitter as it's not what people come to me for. I also don't talk about publishing or book marketing on my JFPenn.com website or Facebook Page.

One word of warning. It's easy to become addicted to email and social media and the immediacy of being wanted. But to create, you need time away from other people. As Jocelyn Glei says in *Manage your Day to Day*, "It's better to disappoint a few people over small things, than to surrender your dreams for an empty inbox."

Decide on the line you won't cross

There are obviously some things that are important to keep private. Perhaps you will never share pictures of your family. I generally don't and since my husband and I don't share a last name, I keep him separate from my author persona. Some authors I know make up code names for their kids so they can talk about them without invading their privacy. You need to decide where your line is and then share authentically while still protecting yourself.

"Be you because others are taken."

Oscar Wilde

2.6 Haters gonna hate

"I would advise anyone who aspires to a writing career
that before developing his talent he would be wise to
develop a thick hide."

Harper Lee

I used to check my email in the morning. It's a bad practice as it puts the world on your agenda and things can set you off emotionally, things that will stay in your head for way too long. I've had hate mail, like most people with an online presence, but this particular email came in once that bothered me.

Perhaps it bothers me still.

"You're tepid and banal," the email said, followed by a litany of things I had supposed erred on.

Now perhaps you don't think that is offensive, but we all have our cracks and this one slithered through mine and it sprang to mind as the example I wanted to share in this chapter because I aim to be extraordinary in my life. Calling me tepid really makes me mad!

Of course, there are trolls and crazies and haters and many of those may even be other authors, driven by jealousy. But most of us (luckily) don't get death threats or serious hate mail. Instead, it will be the one-star reviews that get you, or emails like that one.

In over eight years with an online platform, 99.99999% of my online interaction has been happy and positive.

However, if you write about 'hot button' topics, you're likely to get some reaction from readers, and if you make it into the big leagues, you'll get your share of haters, because that's what happens to famous people. I heard Charlaine Harris (author of the Sookie Stackhouse series that became True Blood) interviewed by top crime writer Karin Slaughter at ThrillerFest and they both talked at length about being careful around fans. They mentioned never eating anything a fan gives them … just in case. Charlaine has a secret word for her assistant in case she needs a fast exit and never lets people behind her at events/signings. There are problems are every level of the author journey, so be careful what you wish for! You have to get out there among the fans, but you still need to protect yourself, too.

The more successful you are, the more people will attack you.

Your challenge is not to react.

If you react in public, you may be seen as the person in the wrong, whatever the truth behind it all. It also feeds the flames of whatever has been said and gives oxygen to the story. If you don't respond, it will die away more quickly.

Antidote:

Understand that this may happen at some point. You can't insulate yourself completely unless you don't publish anything, ever. If you want success as an author, then this is the trade-off. People will attack you eventually, so be ready and have your strategy in place.

It's human nature to notice the negative comments more than the positive, the one-star reviews rather than the four and five-star. But as an author, you will also get fan mail. People will email you and say they love your books. They will leave lovely reviews on Goodreads and Amazon or other sites. Don't just read and dismiss these emails. Print them out and stick them in a folder or journal. Email them to Evernote or save them in a folder on your computer marked Fan Mail. Read when you're miserable or feeling attacked and it will make a real difference.

Don't engage with trolls or haters. Don't give them air. Get off the Internet and go for a long walk. Take some deep breaths and consider what is really important in your life.

The people who love you and who you want to spend time with.

Your health.

Your creative body of work.

Your sanity.

If it gets difficult, consider getting a separate email for your author life and employ a virtual assistant to check your email and social media. Give them specific instructions for what to do e.g. delete, block, report, and make them the filter. Don't let it get inside your head. Haters gonna hate, so just keep creating.

2.7 Ambition, fame and fortune

"To feel ambition and to act upon it is to embrace the unique calling of our souls."

Steven Pressfield

In the first chapter, I described a panel at ThrillerFest in New York with a panel of seven authors at the top of the writing game including R.L.Stine, Clive Cussler, Lee Child and Sandra Brown. As they spoke, I thought, "I want to be up there. I want to be that successful. I want that many people to love my writing – and yes, I want that kind of money and fame."

That's ego talking.

That's ambition talking.

And there's nothing wrong with that.

Perhaps writers without ego end up journaling, or maybe ghostwriting. Because you need a healthy ego to want your writing to be published and available for the world to read and judge.

But ambition is a difficult topic for many writers and few will admit to it.

So I will!

I'm ambitious. I want to see my books made into movies, games and virtual reality worlds. I want to be on the Forbes

Richest Author List, not so much for the money (although of course that's great!), but more for the recognition that it means millions of readers enjoy my books. I don't want to be mid-list. I want to be a name brand author. My role model is Stephen King and my ambition is to have hundreds of thousands, even millions, of readers around the world say that my books are the ones they remember the most.

I want to write a book as memorable as *The Stand* by Stephen King or *The Source* by James Michener, which both changed the way I think and write. I want to stand out creatively, and this part of my ambition keeps me writing the books I love and not chasing the market or the money, even though this ambition will clearly take some time!

At the other end of the scale, I recently interviewed literary and historical fiction writer, Libbie Hawker. Her ambition is to win a Pulitzer Prize for her literary work. It was great to meet another ambitious author who is not afraid to state big goals.

Listen to the interview here:

www.TheCreativePenn.com/libbie

Both of our ambitions are long-term and both of us are looking to hit those goals in the next 25 to 30 years, although sooner would be great! In the meantime, we both focus on the short-term goals of words on the page, the next chapter, the next book, as well as continuing to learn the writing craft and building our audiences.

Think big for a moment.

What are your writing ambitions?

How much do you want to achieve them?

> "If you want success, figure out the price, then pay it."
>
> *Scott Adams, creator of Dilbert*

So how do we achieve these ambitions? Or even take steps toward them.

By writing more, that's how. New stories, new books, new ideas, new worlds.

Not blogging, or podcasting or hanging out on social media. But through writing. You can't write for 15 minutes a day and expect to be an international bestseller. Ambitious authors have to work hard, but hey, what else do you want to do with your time?

> "We really have no idea how deep our reservoir runs, no clear estimate of where our limits lie."
>
> *Steven Kotler, The Rise of Superman*

What if you hit the top? What if you achieve all your goals?

Let's hear the answer from Elizabeth Gilbert whose book, *Eat, Pray, Love*, became a massive bestseller, a hit movie, and made sure she was financially set for life. People asked her afterwards what it felt like to have reached the pinnacle of her career, implying that it was all downhill from that point.

"Even if you get to the top, you will instantly fall again. You never stay at the top for long. The work itself is the reward. The quiet glory of making things."

Elizabeth Gilbert, Big Magic

2.8 Giving up

"If at first you don't succeed, try, try again. Then quit.
There's no point in being a damn fool about it."

W. C. Fields

Writing changes its meaning to our lives over time. Here's how writing has changed for me over the years.

When I was 15, writing a journal was my way to navigate a difficult time of life. The blank page was my confidante and friend, the way I figured out the world – or at least, how I survived it.

At 28 and going through a divorce, writing was a way to heal myself, to purge my anger and pain until the power drained out of the experience and I was whole again. I read those words now and I don't even recognize that woman, because I left it all behind on the page.

When I wrote my first non-fiction book at 32, writing was a way to change my own life and hopefully that of others. My first novel was another shift, a way to explore what I thought by way of story. In all these years, writing was something I fought for time to indulge in, an almost guilty pleasure on the side of 'real life.'

Then at 36, I left my day job to make a living with my writing and it morphed into something more complicated. Because if you write to pay the bills, and the term 'author' is bound up in your self-image and how others perceive you, then writing is no longer just a retreat and a haven. It can still be that, and indeed I still journal regularly, but it is also a way to put food on the table and pay the mortgage. You may end up driven to the page by necessity, rather than a deep desire to express what's in your mind.

And that can be a problem.

At this point, I can't see any other way I want to spend my life, because I enjoy every part of the author life – the business side as well as the creative. But I know many authors who have given up writing books, or are considering it, because it has become just another job.

Some are burned out by the struggle to fulfill contractual obligations to a publisher, or meet the demands of editors who want a specific type of book that the author just isn't inspired by. Others don't like the aspects of the author life that don't involve time alone creating, because however you publish these days, you will need to market your books and manage the business side. Many more just feel that the pitiful financial rewards don't make it worth the time to continue writing professionally, preferring to stop altogether than weather the pain of the mid-list.

Antidote:

First of all, don't feel guilty if you are thinking of giving up writing books. The writer's life is not for everyone, and if writing is just another job, then consider that many people change careers in a lifetime, so it's inevitable that some decide to pursue other paths.

Take a step back and evaluate why you feel like this

Really be honest with yourself and try to work out what is causing this feeling. Why did you want to write a book in the first place? When did you lose that drive and those ideas?

Are you really completely finally done with writing? Or perhaps you're just burned out and overwhelmed and need a break before trying again?

Take a break

Withdraw as much as possible from social media and all the noise that says what it's meant to be like as a writer. Finish any obligations and just get on with real life for a bit. Let any feelings of guilt and failure go, and chances are, after a break, you will find words bubbling out of you again somehow.

Also, stop taking yourself so seriously! I meet way too many writers who get wound up by the need to write something literary and important, whereas if you write things that you are interested in or are excited about, then you will regain your energy. This is also why a lot of indie authors are so empowered and happy, because we write the book first and then try to sell it, retaining creative control, whereas many traditionally published authors are writing subsequent books post debut to order, even if they're not inspired by the idea anymore.

Go back to a day job and write for pleasure

Most authors have a day job anyway, so this is for those who have left their jobs to write full-time and then discovered that it is not all it's cracked up to be. The pressure of having to earn money with your writing can sometimes be the thing that kills it, or the pressure to hit a list or to reach some standard set by the community we are part of. Take away the pressure to earn and you may find your writing mojo again. Chances are you will carry on writing something, even just birthday cards! But maybe it's time to take a little break from the treadmill of publishing.

Part 3:
Tips for Success on the Author Journey

3.1 Know thyself

"Know thyself."

Inscription on the Temple of Apollo at Delphi

There's a great deal of self-knowledge involved in writing, because we spend countless hours with our own minds pondering the secrets of our books and committing our thoughts to the page. Perhaps we even come to know what we think through writing it, which is certainly my own experience. If there's a topic or theme or question in my mind, I write a book about it in order to know what I think.

But it's also important to understand yourself when it comes to the other aspects of being an author, because many of the issues that authors face stem from not being clear about motivation and your definition of success, for example, the literary author who constantly complains about lack of sales and income, or the genre fiction author who complains about not being accepted for prizes or lack of attention from literary festivals or media. This comes back to definition of success, covered in chapter 2.2.

Hopefully, this book also helps with knowing yourself in terms of the psychological journey, because the storms of the creative process can derail us unless we understand that they are just part of the way forward.

Map your own creative energy cycles

What are the parts of the writing process that you love? What can't you wait to get on with? Conversely, what drains you and makes you negatively exhausted?

Personally, I'm a research junkie and will happily spend days lost in libraries, on research trips and in weird corners of the Internet digging up interesting things for my books. I also love the wrangling aspect of structure, and the emergence of ideas that I didn't even know were in my mind until I write. I'm addicted to the satisfaction of finishing a book, of completing a task and being able to say, "I made that." Spending time alone recharges me, and if that resonates, I recommend you read *Quiet* by Susan Cain, which helped me understand why I need so much alone time.

In terms of what drains me, I can't cope with multi-day events like festivals and conferences unless I have a lot of recharge time between sessions. Too many people is too stressful, so nowadays I try to only attend for one day, or make sure I can get away to my hotel room or somewhere else quiet for time alone.

Once you understand what energizes you and what drains you, you'll be able to map your creative life so that it sustains you long term.

"You and I, who are artists and entrepreneurs, live a life that's closer to natural … We migrate. We follow the Muse instead of the sun."

Steven Pressfield, Turning Pro

I find natural metaphors for creativity to be a great relief because there is a sense of ebb and flow about them. We cannot expect to be at the peak of creativity all the time. We need those seasonal breaks, those fallow times when the mind can rest and recharge. I also like the idea of the creative project as coming to fruition, then we pick that crop and move onto the next thing. That harvest goes into the world and we are then disconnected from it. Of course, that emotional distance from our creation is something I am still working on!

You are likely to have a daily ebb and flow – times when you feel ready for anything and times when you need rest. I'm a morning person, so I am raring to create first thing, but by about 3pm, I'm done and need to move onto other things like marketing or business stuff. Prolific bestselling authors Dean Wesley Smith and Kristine Kathryn Rusch are night owls, starting their creative work well into the night and working until the early hours. It doesn't matter what your daily energy patterns are, you just need to understand them.

You'll also have a weekly ebb and flow around your day job and family commitments, and you could map what works best for you at that level. Then take it further and look at the months ahead for the whole year. I love New Year and have immense energy in January, but I know that December is always a tough month for me. I need to cut myself some slack and relax more when my energy is spent and wait for it to return again.

You can also think of this ebb and flow as a creative cycle across larger swathes of time. If you find yourself dry and blocked for a time, don't fret too much. Expect the rain to come again and the cycle to continue.

This too shall pass.

What do you really want?

If you don't actively decide what you want to do with your life, then you may wake up one day and wonder how you ended up where you are. That happened to me with my first career and it took years to change direction and get to a point where I am truly happy with my choices.

So spend some time working on understanding yourself and admitting the truth of what you really want, beneath the veneer of what's expected by others. Ask yourself the hard questions about what makes you happy, what drags you down, what will help you to achieve your five year goals, and how you might get there.

Don't censor yourself and don't put limits on your dreams. Ten years ago I could not have comprehended living the creative life I do now, but looking back, I can see how each tiny decision toward what I really wanted made a difference.

> "Whatever excites you, go do it. Whatever drains you, stop doing it."
>
> *Derek Sivers*

3.2 Understand and hone your creative process

"Big success comes when we do a few things well. You need to be doing fewer things for more effect."

Gary Keller, The One Thing

When we first begin to write, before any thought of publication or career, we go to the blank page based on an inner urge, a desire to pour out something within. That urge is like the attraction to a lover, one we are desperate to spend more time with. But in becoming a professional writer, we need to write when that urge isn't present. For sure, it still comes sometimes, whirling us into ecstasy, but the life of a professional writer is more like a marriage with creativity, when process and routine are more important than an occasional passionate encounter that is too soon finished and spent.

Each of us has our own creative process, but until you understand yours, you may find yourself flailing around at the start of every book, or even within it. You might feel a resistance to this codification of something that seems uncatchable somehow, but it will simplify your life and allow more time for your mind to spend creating.

Here's an extract from my journal in March 2010 as I wrote my first novel while still working the day job:

"I had a marvelous day writing today. I immersed myself in the topic, did some mind-maps and research and wrote 3,500 words. I wasn't distracted, just focused. What's the key to getting into this state? I need to know so that I can repeat it.

- **Mulching time:** I've been thinking a lot about the plot and ideas, sleeping on it, and my subconscious has had time to play. My characters are solidifying and as I learn more, I can see the novel coming together.

- **Concentrated effort:** no distractions for a few hours. I listened to rain and thunderstorms on repeat to enable deeper concentration.

- **Being ready to write:** I felt frustrated that I haven't written all week, but today I made up for it.

- **Writing before I do anything else:** I can't write creatively in the evenings as my brain has exploded from other work, so I need to write in the mornings before I get distracted by everything else.

- **Think of writing time are playtime:** It's fun making stuff up! Don't buy into your own hype. 'My writing is SO important!' This stifles my inner creative child."

This was the start of discovering how my creative process works, or at least the writing part. Back then, I was still working on Microsoft Word, but now I use Scrivener software, which is one of the biggest improvements in my process, as it helps the writer organize and wrangle ideas. I use it to set up scenes or chapters using one-liners before writing the first draft, and for a mini-outline for the biggest high points of the book, but mainly, I make it up as I go along.

My mantra is: Trust emergence.

Something will come when I go to the page.

I still write creatively in the mornings and I still listen to rain and thunderstorms to get into a concentrated state. I tend to write new words in cafes or libraries, away from my home office where I do all the other things that go into running a creative business. I'm sitting in a cafe right now with my trusty cup of coffee to hand. I also dictate at my standing desk or out walking. I will typically do two hours and then move somewhere else to get some fresh air en route and then do another two hours, which is usually all I can manage in one session.

My editing process is also clear now. My first draft is finished when someone could read the whole thing end to end as a coherent book, with nothing missing like "Insert action scene here." I print out the first draft and then edit by hand, again usually in cafes. I then make the changes into Scrivener and add in what I need to, rewrite and fix. Then I print and edit by hand again. Sometimes the book is ready at this point and I can send it to a professional editor, but sometimes I'll need to repeat that process until it's done.

I use different editors for fiction and non-fiction and then make editorial changes before using a proofreader before publication. I sometimes use beta-readers for specific topics, e.g. for dark fantasy thriller *Risen Gods*, which is based in New Zealand with erupting volcanoes and Maori mythology, I had a vulcanologist and a Maori beta reader to check for any issues.

It's also important to notice and acknowledge the psychological journey that you go through as part of the creative process. It can be frustrating to try and wrangle huge ideas, or to struggle to find the time to write, or to knit together parts of a book that just don't seem to gel. Perhaps you want to tear your hair out over edits! But remember, as Elizabeth Gilbert says in *Big Magic*, "Frustration is not an interruption of your process; frustration *is* the process."

The experience you have while writing and who you become over that time is the point. Pushing through frustration to success, celebrating those small wins of words written or chapters finished is perhaps the most important part of the journey. You are changing your mind and maybe your life and those of others through what you write. There is definitely something mystical in what we do, but it only happens if we can commit to working out a sustainable process that keeps us creating for the long term.

"Be regular and orderly in your life, so that you may be violent and original in your work."

Gustave Flaubert

3.3 Develop professional habits

"Don't wait for the muse ... Your job is to make sure the muse knows where you're going to be every day from 9 until noon or 7 'til 3. If he does know, I assure you that sooner or later he'll start showing up, chomping his cigar and making his magic."

Stephen King

It all comes down to this fundamental thing: Writers write.

How they write is where everyone differs and, of course, there is no correct way to get black on white. What's important is that it happens at all, and this can be helped by developing professional habits around the creative process.

Studies show that we only have a certain amount of will-power to spend every day, and that the best thing to do is automate things so that you have to make fewer decisions. Habits remove the need to make decisions. You just do them because that's part of your routine, like brushing your teeth. Read *The Power of Habit* by Charles Duhigg for more on this.

What are your good habits right now that help you achieve your writing goals?

And what are your bad habits?

Here are some of my tips for developing professional habits.

Schedule your writing time and do it even if you feel like crap

The secret to my own productivity is my trusty Filofax diary, which I bought with my first official pay check back in the 1990s. I block out chunks of time for writing months in advance and then schedule other things around it, like research trips, interviews, publication and marketing tasks, as well as real-life stuff. Then I keep those writing appointments, as I would any other official meeting. Before I go to bed each night, I will briefly write out what needs to be done the next day, and it will include the writing task. I don't take for granted that I will just do it, because it's likely that I won't unless I specifically schedule time.

You also need to show up for the writing session even if you are feeling like crap, just as you would get to your day job unless you were really, really sick. As fantasy author Neil Gaiman said, "Something you write with a headache is as good as something you write when you're feeling fine." I've seen the truth of this over the years, and it still surprises me. Some chapters in a book can be written in a state of flow, when everything comes easily and your fingers flash over the keyboard. Others are written like molasses, slowly dripping onto the page. But when you read the book later, you can't tell what was written when. Your feelings don't affect the finished product, *if* you put in the time to write.

Balance Maker time and Manager time

One of the most common questions that I get asked is how to balance writing and marketing.

First of all, we are creatives first and you will eventually be driven back to the page by that internal sense that you need to write. I get grumpy if I've not been writing enough and often feel relief when I can just have time alone to write. But if I've let it get that far, I know I've been distracted too much by other things that might seem important, but are likely things that won't last and won't impact my body of work.

Then you need to consider Maker time (when you create) vs. Manager time (when you do everything else associated with being an author). This concept was first articulated by Paul Graham, programmer and founder of tech startup incubator, Y Combinator, where companies like AirBnB and Dropbox originated.

Say no to distraction when you are in Maker mode.

Distractions during Maker time might include blogging, Twitter and Facebook. They are not inherently bad, they just distract us from our true purpose as we head down a rabbit hole on the Internet, losing hours in the process, or when we focus on watching what others are doing instead of creating our own art.

As Steven Pressfield says in *Turning Pro*, "Resistance hates concentration and depth ... Resistance wants to keep us shallow and unfocused. So it makes the shallow and superficial intoxicating."

But why is this so hard to do?

Have you checked your email in the last half an hour? Are you addicted to your smart phone or tablet? Do you crave that social media hit?

I'll admit to struggling with this as much as anyone, and there's only one way to deal with it. Turn off email, Twitter, Facebook and anything else distracting during your Maker time. Turn off all notifications on your devices. Use a computer with no Internet access if necessary and put your phone on airplane mode. Put headphones on and play whatever helps to dull ambient noise so you can concentrate.

Because there is no such thing as multi-tasking.

There is only task-switching, which means that your depth of concentration is broken, and the Muse won't tolerate these distractions. There are no rules, but you need to find your own way to focus and go deeper into your own creative concentration. For more on this, check out *Deep Work* by Cal Newport.

Every day we have to make the decision to be a professional writer with professional habits. There will be days when we will lose. No one said this was easy! But over time, as we develop the habit, we will find ourselves winning more days than not.

"On the field of the self stand a knight and a dragon. You are the knight. Resistance is the dragon. The battle must be fought anew every day."

Steven Pressfield, The War of Art

Say "no" more

This goes even further than saying no to distraction. It's about saying no to external events and people, which is something that I struggle with all the time. I want to be helpful and useful to my community and I also want to participate in all the events online and in real life. I want to socialize and I want to travel more and see friends and join in whatever interesting thing that's happening right now.

But the more you become known, the more these opportunities arise, and the more you have to say no, because there is only so much time, and if all of that time is taken up with other people and other things, then your own creative work won't happen, and by the end of the year, you'll wonder what the hell happened to your time. You can end up building a trap for yourself with other people's expectations and end up resenting what you've committed to.

I love speaking and inspiring people, but as an introvert, when I connect too much and speak too often, I break down, so I need to make sure I don't speak too often. I want to reply to all the emails I get, but it eats minutes from the day, and isn't it better to have a book like this than spend the same amount of time writing two-line emails to hundreds of people? So I try to share and help others through the blog, podcast, books and courses. I also want to travel all the time because I hate staying still and moving seems to be my natural state, but if I am constantly distracted by new and exciting places, I never have time to reflect and write about the experiences.

Decide what is important and schedule that time first (writing!) and then look at what time is left for the other things. I used to feel happy if my schedule was filled with appointments, but now I realize that it's much more effective to have weeks of white space, because that's when creativity emerges. I'm trying to break my own connection between 'busy' and productive formed by years in corporate work, because that's not how the creative process works best. More empty time actually means more creativity. More busy time means more stuff on other people's agendas.

What do you need to say no to?

> "Be as generous as you can, but selfish
> enough to protect your work."
>
> *Austin Kleon*

3.4 Manage professional relationships

This section can be summed up in one line that I heard from author and podcaster Mur Lafferty on her *I Should Be Writing* podcast many years ago in reference to behaving like a professional author.

"Don't be a dick."

It should be self-evident that it's important to maintain professional relationships with agents, editors, publishers, professional freelancers, bloggers, other authors and most importantly, readers, but it's surprising how many authors seem to forget this, especially in an online world.

Writing is a long-term game and over the years, you are likely to run into the same people in the publishing industry. Agents and editors may move companies, but they will remember what you were like, and they all talk amongst themselves. Professional freelancers, like the best cover designers and editors, will only continue to work with those clients who are good to work with and who pay on time.

You will also meet other authors at events or on forums/ private groups and you don't know who that author will be in five years or twenty years. The relationships you make early in your career can stick with you for the long term and you may be able to help each other now and in the future. There will always be people ahead of you and behind you on the author journey, so help who you can and you never know what social karma will come back to you. Generosity makes for a happier life and a giving community. I might not write fiction that is all rainbows and kittens, but I definitely try to live that way!

The word karma implies that you get back what you give, and I believe this is true in the social environment. If you give, you will receive somehow, though not always from the same source. Being useful, helpful and generous is satisfying to you personally, but also builds up a bank of goodwill. When you later mention that you have a book out, or people are attracted to you because of your generosity, and see that you have books/products available, they are more likely to buy.

This isn't woo-woo. It's based on the science of influence. Read Robert Cialdini's book *Influence* and you'll see that the principle of reciprocity is one of the keys to influencing people's behavior. I believe that we can utilize such principles, but we don't have to do it in a scammy or unethical manner.

Co-opetition is the idea of cooperating with your perceived competition so that both parties benefit. When there is a congruence of interests, cooperating together can create greater value than acting alone. The self-publishing environment in particular is full of entrepreneurial authors, sharing openly. We discuss sales numbers and promote each other through blog posts and social networks, especially when our books are in the same genre. In working and educating ourselves together, we can learn lessons faster, respond and adapt more quickly. Traditionally published authors also do this through promoting each other's books, forming groups that speak together at festivals or doing book signings together.

For example, let's say you write science fiction. There's no need to see other science fiction writers as competition. Instead, think of them as potential collaborators on marketing projects. Both of you bring an interested group of readers who will read your books fast and be ready for the next book. Why not work with other writers in the same genre to promote each other? In that way, everyone benefits. In the same way, non-fiction writers can work with authors in the same area to target the same readers. After all, a reader who buys one diet book will likely want to buy a whole load more of them!

Perception is also important when it comes to being professional. Anything that has your name on it should bolster your reputation, not diminish it. Anything that you share in a supposedly private forum or Facebook group may be screen-grabbed and shared, or talked about by others. Even if what you say is justified, if things make it into the blogosphere or social media, you may be the one left looking bad. So if you're boiling over with anger and want to lash out, don't blog or tweet or Facebook about it, deal with it privately if possible to protect your own brand.

Respond to reader emails graciously and gratefully, because they are the ones who make a success of your book. If you meet fans at events, smile and be nice. A stand-offish author with no time for readers soon gets a reputation. Perhaps that doesn't impact sales in the short term, but reader opinion is often shared across blog networks and social media over time.

"Be nice to people on the way up because you'll meet them on the way down."

Wilson Mizner

3.5 Take control of your writing career

"Set a goal that is big enough that in the process of achieving it you become someone worth becoming."

Jim Rohn

No one cares about your life as much as you do, and no one will care about your author career as much as you do over the many years it will hopefully last. If you have breakout success with a book, then sure, you will have lots of people who care very much what happens, as their pay checks will depend upon it, but for most authors, the writing career is what *you* make of it and the main reward is the creative work and the journey itself.

So how can you take control?

Make sure you are working toward what you really want

"I don't want to write another book in this crime series, but my agent says it's what will sell," my author friend sighs. "I'm blocked for ideas and resisting writing because I'm just not interested anymore." She takes a sip of wine. "There is something else I want to write, though." Her eyes light up as she describes a creative project that has nothing to do with the established series that currently earns her money.

Should she write the book her agent wants? Or try the passion project and see how that goes?

The answer depends on the author and what they really want for the long term.

> "Branding is important and takes a long time to build. Make sure that the brand you construct is what you really want to do. Because once you've built it, it's hard to change."
>
> *Bob Mayer*

I saw this happening with *Career Change*, the first non-fiction book I wrote. Once it was out and I started to promote it with guest blogging and my own website on escaping the corporate world, I was invited to speak and suddenly realized that I didn't want to spend my life speaking on that topic. Everything I wanted to say was encapsulated in the book and I was ready to move on. After 13 years in a job I never liked and actively hated toward the end, I wasn't willing to spend my time doing work I wasn't passionate about.

So I went back to the fundamentals. What did I really want to do with my life? How did I want to spend my time?

There's a powerful question that I think I first encountered in a Tony Robbins self-help book.

"What is the one word that sums up what you want in life, the core value that will drive your decisions?"

This is not an easy question, but after much deliberation I decided that my word was Freedom. It still guides my life. It's manifest in my decision to travel and move countries, and to choose experiences over owning things. It's why I focus on digital sales and a location-independent business. I don't like asking permission or depending on others so perhaps it's also why I primarily choose to be an independent author.

Your life values and your word will no doubt be different to mine, but if you can identify what you really want, it will help to guide the many decisions you will need to make along the way.

Don't just create another job.

Design the life and the work you really want, because life is all too short.

Set goals and track your progress

Once you decide what you want on a broad level, you can then make that more specific. I go into more detail about doing this in *How to Make a Living with your Writing*, but basically you need to break down your bigger life goals into smaller chunks and more achievable steps. Writing these down in the form of a business plan, blogging about it in public (as I do!) or just journaling it will make a huge difference.

These written goals will help you focus and stay clear on what your priorities are without getting distracted by every new shiny object.

"People with clear written goals accomplish far more in a shorter period of time than people without them could ever imagine."

Brian Tracy

The empowerment of indie

This is not a book about how to publish so I won't go into the specific details here. (Check out my book, *Successful Self-Publishing: How to Self-Publish and Market your Book* if you want more practical information.)

But one of the reasons that I'm an independent author by choice is because of the control I have over my creative work and therefore, my income and lifestyle.

I didn't wait to be picked. I picked myself.

I made mistakes and learned along the way, but I learned much faster by doing it myself and was able to transition out of my day job and make a good living much faster than most traditionally published authors, many of whom are trapped within a mindset of "someone else will do this for me," and the specific demands of producing to contract.

Psychological research shows that people who have agency or control over their situation are happier than those who are at the mercy of outside forces. This 'locus of control' sits with the indie author when you self-publish and your results are dependent on how much you can learn and implement along the way. It's not for everyone, but it might be worth a try.

Because if I hadn't self-published *Stone of Fire* (previously

Pentecost) in 2011, or clicked Publish on my blog, I would likely still be a miserable business consultant, talking about writing but not doing it. If I hadn't persisted through the first three novels, I would not have found my voice in the fourth. If I had asked permission, or if I had waited to be picked, I would still be dreaming of what might have been.

Of course, permission to write and self-publish doesn't mean you'll get it right the first time. It doesn't guarantee Hugh Howey-type success. But it shifts you inside, it forces you to go further creatively. It enables you to clear the way for the next step and, after all, the writer's life is a journey of discovery, not a destination.

So you have permission. You are empowered.

To write. To publish. To connect with readers and writers all over the globe.

Now go write.

> "Indie publishing isn't just changing publishing,
> it's changing writers."
>
> *Susan Kaye Quinn*

3.6 Find your community

"Part of the act of creating is discovering your own kind.
They are everywhere."

Henry Miller

It is said that writing is one of the loneliest professions, that you sit at a desk, alone with your thoughts, and the person reading them eventually is separated from you by time and space. Your family won't understand you and your old friends may drift away as they can't fathom quite how you spend your time.

When first I started writing, I didn't know any authors. I considered 'them' to be a world away from me, and I could never hope to meet them, let alone socialize with them. Nowadays my best friends are authors. I hang out with them at festivals, I interview them on my podcast and we blurb each other's books. My community has shifted from a corporate-centered world to a creative one, so it's definitely possible for you, too.

It is so important to find a community because there will be times you'll want to celebrate with others and times you will be down and need support. Yes, the writing life can be lonely, but due to the magic of the Internet, it doesn't have to be.

Find like minds online

Whether it's Twitter hashtags like #amwriting or forums like KBoards, Facebook or LinkedIn groups, you can find a like-minded bunch of people to hang out and talk about writing and books with online. This will likely be easier than finding people physically near you. The group might be genre-related or topic-focused, related to publishing or book marketing, or organized as an extra around a live event.

There are also professional organizations that have private groups you can join, like the Alliance of Independent Authors, which has a lively Facebook group where anyone can ask questions. There are also groups associated with online courses, like my own private Creative Freedom community.

You can find a group online at any level of the author journey. Just start looking!

Focus on getting to know your peers

If you haven't written a book yet, it's unlikely that you will be able to become part of a community of authors with multiple books, because you just don't have the experience to talk at the level they do. So it's better to build a community of peers. For example, I wouldn't ask Stephen King or J.K. Rowling to join me for a writing group!

Conversely, if you've written five books and are making some decent cash, you probably won't be welcome as part of a beginning writers' group. I discovered this when I tried to join a local writer's group in London and was basically told by the leader that I was 'too advanced' and would make others feel inadequate. I had to laugh, because that's exactly how I feel about authors who are years ahead of me along the path.

My close author friends are now mid-list, traditionally published authors and also professional indie authors, as we can all help each other and share where we are on the journey. I expect that we will grow together over the years and someday, we'll be the new Kings, Rowlings or Pattersons!

Be honest about where you are on the writer's journey and make friends with people at your level. You will also shift over time, for example, 90% of people in your writer's group will never finish a book, but when you do, you will move into a new group of new authors.

Give before you expect to receive

I started my podcast back in 2009 so that I could talk to creative people. I didn't know any, so I decided that the best way was to have something to offer them in the form of a video or audio interview that would help promote them. Otherwise, why would they even bother getting on Skype with me or respond to my email? The podcast has become the cornerstone of my relationships with other authors and if I want to get to know a new person, I will often start by inviting them on the podcast.

Of course, you don't need to start a podcast to make friends with other authors! The same generosity principle applies to buying and reviewing books, doing blog posts about people's books or courses, sharing information about an author on social media or in your newsletter and other ways of promoting others. Yes, you're doing it because you truly think it's great material, but also, you are more likely to get noticed if you consistently promote someone else's work. It will take time, but from my own experience I can tell you that it pays dividends in the long run.

Attend live events

As an introvert, live events are tough for me because they are so draining, but they are also absolutely necessary if you are going to develop friends in the author world. Live events are well worth the time, effort and money and I go to several in the UK and internationally every year.

But I will never go to a conference or event unprepared, otherwise I will end up in my room quiet and alone! Twitter is my secret weapon and I will stalk people online before an event and get to know them through their blog and then use that initial connection to spark a conversation.

If you're just starting out at a conference, open with, "It's my first time here" and you will either bond with another newbie or get some insight into the event from someone who has attended before. If you go back the following year, you will have people you already know. After a number of years of attending, you will have become a fixture, people will recognize you and you'll have a peer group.

I go to a couple of annual conferences and it is definitely daunting in year one. You feel like a nobody and you have no friends. But over time, you develop relationships, and for many authors, these conferences are the key to a supportive network, the essential face time to tide everyone over until next time.

A little warning …

Be careful who you spend your time with, and assess at regular intervals whether you have changed or they have. It may be time to move on from that local critique group or online group.

It can be addictive to hang out in forums, but things can get toxic. Don't be associated with people who just want to be negative and drag others down with them.

> "You are the average of the five people you spend the most time with."
>
> *Jim Rohn*

3.7 Keep learning

"We are all apprentices in a craft where no one ever
becomes a master."

Ernest Hemingway

One of the reasons I love being a writer is that I know I can continue to learn and put new ideas into practice until the day I die. Curiosity is what drives me to the page. Curiosity for what I can discover about the world as I research, and for what I think that only emerges on the page. And of course, if you master one aspect of the craft, there are always myriad more things to discover and try out, and that's exciting!

If you're tired of writing in a particular genre, try something in a different one.

If you don't want to write another 90,000-word thriller or 120,000-word epic fantasy, then chill out and write a 25,000-word novella.

If you need a palette-cleanser after a harrowing novel writing experience, then write some non-fiction.

If you're bored with non-fiction how-to books, write a zombie-post-apocalyptic adventure.

If you're exhausted by your very serious literary fiction, write a sweet romance under another name.

If you're fed up with what your publisher wants you to write, do an indie book in whatever genre you want.

It's your creative life. You get to choose!

We will also keep learning and improving over time.

For some reason, the myth of the publishing industry is of the perfect debut novel that hits the top of the bestseller lists and thus a career is launched. The reality is that authors get better over time, as any professional does, so our early books may be the ones we are embarrassed about later. But hey, you have to get through those in order to improve! As Alain de Botton said, "Anyone who isn't embarrassed of who they were last year probably isn't learning enough."

Learning new skills is also critical in a world that is constantly changing with technology. Even five years ago, authors had a limited choice as to how to make a living with their writing and reach readers with their books. Now, we have so many technologies that help us to publish and market, as well as connect to each other and to readers. Those authors who are willing to learn can be catapulted ahead. Those who resist may well be left behind.

"I am always doing that which I cannot do
in order to learn how to do it."

Pablo Picasso

3.8 Schedule rest and take time off

"Constant doing creates burnout with no space even to know what you want to write – or say."

Natalie Goldberg

I don't know why taking time off has to be emphasized so much to writers. No other profession seems to advocate doing the same thing every day without fail even if it kills you. Even God took a day out to rest after six days of creating, so why can't you?

If you're overwhelmed or you feel like having a social media meltdown or you're sending angry or nasty emails, then take a deep breath and step back.

Turn off your phone and the Internet. Stop reading email and stop following social media.

There will always be more to do. It never stops.

There's never a good time to have a break. So just step away.

Write in order to live, but also to live in order to write

Since September 2011, I've been making a full-time living as an author entrepreneur. It's my passion as well as my income and I write because I love it, as well as to pay the bills. I think work-life balance is something you need if you don't love what you do, so I am a happy workaholic … most of the time!

But we all need inspiration and time for an Artist's Date (see *The Artist's Way* by Julia Cameron) to refresh our creative soul. For me, that is often travel, as I am refreshed by new places and find my inspiration in architecture and culture, in religion and myth. Traveling has always been central to my life and my husband even says I have 'itchy foot syndrome.' I get grumpy if I don't travel enough. I need it to fill my mind with ideas so I can continue to write. It's the way I recharge.

If staying at home is more your thing, then try a digital fast. There's a vibration, a speed we rev up to when we spend too long immersed online. It's addictive, exhilarating, awesome fun – and I believe it's necessary these days – but it's not mandatory all the time. In fact, too much will burn you out super-fast. Schedule your time off as you would do with any job.

"You can't come to a moment of creative insight if you haven't got any mental fuel … Digital Sabbaths are crucial for cognition and for the spirit."

Clive Thompson, Smarter than you Think

3.9 Think long term. Create a body of work

"An overnight success is 10 years in the making."

Tom Clancy

Logically, we know that overnight success is a myth. When we see stories in the media about a particular author who made it big, who seemed to come from nowhere, there are usually years of hard work behind the book that went stratospheric. There are also plenty of authors making a decent living who you have never heard of. Of course, there are always lightning strikes when an author hits a zeitgeist, but that's not something to base a business plan on.

Let's put the time it takes to build an author career into perspective.

I come from the corporate world as many of you will likely do too, and most careers work the same way. When you start your first job, how much are you worth after one year of full-time experience?

After three years?

With five years' experience, you begin to be paid a better wage, manage others and attain some expertise.

But you really start to become useful to a company and paid according to your worth between five and ten years in. And in the time you've been doing your job, other people have left and gone elsewhere. A large part of your success after ten years in any industry is just sticking it out, becoming an expert and putting in your time. You really know what you're doing after ten years.

Why would this be any different for the writing career?

When I finally left my corporate job in 2011 to become a full-time author entrepreneur, my income dropped significantly. But of course it was going to, because I was leaving an industry where I had 13 years of extensive experience that companies would pay a premium for, to join a new industry where I only had a couple of years part-time. It took four more years after that before my income rose to my previous level and since then, it has surpassed my old salary. (For more detail, see my book *How to Make a Living with your Writing.*)

Think about other creative industries.

If you start playing the violin, would you expect to be playing solo at Carnegie Hall the following year? Would you expect to make number one in the pop charts with your first song? How long do you think it takes a musician to get to a point of being paid? Or a painter?

So why consider it to be any different as an author?

In the same way, it takes years of working on your craft to become a better writer and it takes years to build up an audience in any niche.

Why expect your first book to be the best thing you'll ever write? Surely your fifth book, or your tenth book, will be better than your first? So get the first one out of your system and move onto the next and the next.

For more experienced writers, is it logical to expect that your trajectory will always be stepping upwards? That every book you write will be a bigger hit than the one before? That your income will go up every year?

Keep creating

On a recent trip to Spain, I visited the Picasso Museum in Malaga, where the artist was born. The exhibition contained drawings, pottery, paintings and sculpture from his early years in the 1890s all the way through to the 1970s. Picasso died at aged 91 and created throughout his whole life. There are estimates that he created over 50,000 pieces of art, only a few of which are known as masterpieces, but you don't create masterpieces without being prolific and continuing with the process of creation over time. Consider prolific authors like Isaac Asimov, Enid Blyton, Nora Roberts or R.L.Stine. You can probably name a handful of their books, but all have written several hundred each. You don't know what the big stuff will be, you don't know which book will take off. Angry Birds was Rovio's fifty-second game.

Whatever you create, you just have to keep putting it out there.

The Picasso exhibition was powerful because the artist's development was clear, the early pieces and sketches as he experimented and learned his craft were obviously just part of the process toward mastery. His doodles and playful work were just as interesting as his finished pieces, even though they might be considered amateur and not actually very 'good.' In fact, the visual art world is excellent at recognizing and valuing an artist's development, allowing for change over the years, whereas the literary world seems obsessed with debut authors making huge deals with their first books. But of course, as with anything, you will get better as you practice and create more over time.

"You learn how to make your work by making your work, and a great many pieces along the way will never stand out as finished art. The best you can do is make art you care about – and lots of it!"

David Bayles & Ted Orland, Art and Fear

The magic of intellectual property over the long term

Picasso was an artist but he was also a businessman and liked living well. It's said that he burned some of his early canvases to keep warm in his garret, but he was worth over US$500 million when he died and he left some of the world's greatest art. People laud the starving, crazy artists like Van Gogh, but Picasso might be a better role model for the aspiring wealthy creative entrepreneur. Because the magic of intellectual property assets can only happen by creating work over a long period of time to allow for compounding.

Here's how it works:

- Every book you create is an asset and can put money in your pocket for the long term

- It is scalable, meaning you spend the time to create the book once and it can sell thousands, even millions of times

- You can turn that one manuscript into different formats e.g. ebook, print, audiobook to expand your sales

- You can sell those formats in 190 different countries (I've currently sold English language books in 72 countries as an indie author) and expand your sales even more

- You can license the rights to that asset in multiple ways e.g. selling the print rights, translation rights, film, TV, gaming and other media rights

- These assets can go on earning you money for your whole lifetime plus 70 years after you die according to copyright law (and if your estate is managed well)

The tragedy is that most authors don't see their manuscript as valuable, because they don't see this long-term earning potential. They take short-term cash in hand now rather than letting their intellectual asset base grow over time, compounding as it goes.

Because every new book I publish grows my audience and gives my readers something else to buy. Every book I put out expands my income in these multiple ways. This is the business model that convinced me that I could far surpass the income from my day job as a full-time writer creating my own assets for the long term. It's a creatively satisfying life, but it can be a very profitable one too!

I go into this in a lot more detail in my book, *Business for Authors: How to be an Author Entrepreneur.*

"You cannot have everything in the present. You will have to keep your focus on five to ten years down the road when you will reap the rewards."

Robert Greene, Mastery

What do you want your legacy to be?

From my journal, 22 Oct 2011, a few weeks after quitting my day job.

"I want to make a difference. I want to write something worth writing. I want to last. Yes, I want to entertain, but more than that, I want to be remembered. I want to leave a legacy. I feel like I'm waking up at the moment. That I've been asleep for the last 13 years. Because everything I've done up to now has disappeared. It's time to change that. I will measure my life by what I create."

Pro writers write, and keep writing over time. The successful professional writers have multiple books that they continue to produce, even when previous book sales didn't perform as they would have liked. Professionals aren't put off by short-term disappointment. They produce a body of work over time. They don't believe that one book is a special snowflake and give up when it doesn't hit the mainstream. They know that each page is a development in a journey. The habit is creating every day.

What can you create today that will build your body of work?

"Consistent impact over the course of your life on a body of work you care about deeply is legacy."

Pamela Slim, Body of Work

Life is short. Make the most of it.

In the last six months as I write this, a number of famous actors, musicians and authors have died including David Bowie, Alan Rickman and Prince. Prince's death hit me hard, maybe because his music played in the background of my teens and twenties and I sure partied like it was 1999 back then. But he was an incredible musician, songwriter and all-round creative who lived for his work. Fantasy author Terry Pratchett's death from Alzheimers also made me determined to create more, because death is a certainty. The only question is when.

So what can we do with our time on this earth to be remarkable, to be extraordinary?

CREATE.

That is all we can do. For this body will crumble and die but we are not tethered by it.

Measure your life by what you create.

Now go write.

Conclusion

Thanks for joining me on this journey through the author mindset, and I hope that you can breathe a sigh of relief after reading this book.

Because you're not alone on the writer's journey.

The thoughts and feelings that rise and fall are experienced by everyone who is on the creative path at different points along the way. By pulling back the curtain and acknowledging the complexity in the mind behind the words on a page, I hope I've comforted you with what you've read.

So what's next?

At the end of the day (and the book), it all comes back to writing. So go create today, and if you see someone sitting in your local cafe scribbling in a journal or tapping away on their laptop, maybe give them a little smile.

Because you know what they're going through.

Thank you

Thank you for joining me in this journey through the author mindset. If you found it useful, I'd really appreciate a review or a share on social media. It really helps people to discover the book!

**Want to learn how to write, publish
and market your book?**

Get your free Author 2.0 Blueprint and video series at:
www.TheCreativePenn.com/blueprint

Love audio?

Check out The Creative Penn podcast on
iTunes and Stitcher.

www.TheCreativePenn.com/podcasts

Weekly interviews on writing, publishing, book marketing and creative entrepreneurship.

You can also tweet me @thecreativepenn or join my Facebook Page www.facebook.com/TheCreativePenn.

Bibliography

This list contains books and podcasts that I have used within the book, or that I have found useful in the specific context of topics covered in this book.

Books

On Writing - Stephen King

Bird by Bird: Some Instructions on Writing and Life - Anne Lamott

Writing Down the Bones - Natalie Goldberg

Wild Mind - Natalie Goldberg

Big Magic: Creative Living Beyond Fear - Elizabeth Gilbert

The War of Art: Break Through your Blocks and Win your Creative Battles - Steven Pressfield

Turning Pro: Tap your Inner Power and Create your Life's Work - Steven Pressfield

Anything you Want - Derek Sivers

The Success Principles: How to get from Where you are to Where you Want to be - Jack Canfield

The Pursuit of Perfection and How it Harms Writers - Kristine Kathryn Rusch

Ignore Everybody and 39 Other Keys to Creativity - Hugh Macleod

Choose Yourself - James Altucher

The Compound Effect - Darren Hardy

The Successful Novelist - David Morrell

Write it Forward - Bob Mayer

Art and Fear: Observations on the Perils (and Rewards) of Artmaking - David Bayles & Ted Orland,

The Gifts of Imperfection: Let go of who you Think you're Supposed to be and Embrace who you are - Brené Brown

Steal Like An Artist - Austin Kleon

The One Thing - Gary Keller

The Art of Asking, or How I Learned to Stop Worrying and Let People Help - Amanda Palmer

Make Art, Make Money: Lessons from Jim Henson on Fueling your Creative Career - Elizabeth Hyde Stevens

The Icarus Deception - Seth Godin

Manage your Day to Day: Build your Routine, Find your Focus and Sharpen your Creative Mind - 99U, edited by Jocelyn Glei

Tiny Beautiful Things - Cheryl Strayed

Zen in the Art of Writing - Ray Bradbury

The Artist's Way - Julia Cameron

The View from the Cheap Seats: Selected Non-Fiction - Neil Gaiman

Resilience: Facing Down Criticism and Rejection on the Road to Success - Mark McGuinness

F-R-E-E Writing: Unblocking Life's Flow - Orna Ross

Deep Work - Cal Newport

Heinlein's Rules - Dean Wesley Smith

If You Want to Write: A Book about Art, Independence and Spirit - Brenda Ueland

On Writing Well - William Zinsser

The Last Lecture - Randy Pausch

Quiet: The Power of Introverts in a World that Can't Stop Talking - Susan Cain

The Power of Habit: Why we do What we do, and How to Change - Charles Duhigg

Smarter than you Think: How Technology is Changing our Minds for the Better - Clive Thompson

Indie Author Survival Guide - Susan Kaye Quinn

Influence: The Psychology of Persuasion - Robert Cialdini

Choosing a Self-Publishing Service - Edited by Orna Ross, published by the Alliance of Independent Authors

Podcasts

Unemployable

The Tim Ferriss Show

On Being with Christa Tippett

I Should Be Writing with Mur Lafferty

Other Books by Joanna Penn

Get your FREE Successful Author Blueprint
and video series:

www.TheCreativePenn.com/blueprint

More Books for Writers

How to Make a Living with Your Writing:
Books, Blogging and More

Successful Self-Publishing:
How to publish an ebook and a print book

How to Market a Book

The Successful Author Mindset

Public Speaking for Authors,
Creatives, and Other Introverts

Co-Writing a Book: Collaboration and
Co-creation for Writers

Business for Authors: How to be an Author Entrepreneur

Career Change: Stop Hating your Job, Discover
What you Really Want to Do, and Start Doing It

How to Write Non-Fiction

* * *

Thrillers by J.F.PENN

Get a free thriller: www.JFPenn.com/free

ARKANE Thrillers

Stone of Fire #1
Crypt of Bone #2
Ark of Blood #3
One Day in Budapest #4
Day of the Vikings #5
Gates of Hell #6
One Day in New York #7
Destroyer of Worlds #8
End of Days #9
Valley of Dry Bones #10

London Crime Thrillers

Desecration #1
Delirium #2
Deviance #3

Mapwalker Dark Fantasy series

Map of Shadows #1

Standalone Fantasy Thrillers

Risen Gods - with J.Thorn

A Thousand Fiendish Angels:
Short Stories Inspired by Dante's Inferno

The Dark Queen:
An Archaeological Short Story

American Demon Hunters: Sacrifice
- with J. Thorn, Lindsay Buroker, Zach Bohannon

About Joanna Penn

Joanna Penn is an Award-nominated, New York Times and USA Today bestselling author of thrillers under J.F.Penn and also writes non-fiction for authors. She's an award-winning entrepreneur, podcaster, and YouTuber.

Her site, TheCreativePenn.com has been voted in the Top 100 sites for writers by Writer's Digest. Joanna also has a popular podcast for writers, The Creative Penn.

Joanna has a Master's degree in Theology from the University of Oxford, Mansfield College, and a Graduate Diploma in Psychology from the University of Auckland, New Zealand.

She lives in Bath, England but spent 11 years living in Australia and New Zealand. Joanna enjoys traveling as often as possible. She's interested in religion and psychology and loves to read, drink gin and tonic, and soak up European culture through art, architecture and food.

Connect with Joanna:

www.TheCreativePenn.com
joanna@TheCreativePenn.com
Twitter: @thecreativepenn
Facebook.com/TheCreativePenn
YouTube.com/thecreativepenn
Instagram.com/JFPennAuthor

Acknowledgments

Thanks to my blog and podcast community at The Creative Penn, as well as those on my email list and on social media. Your encouragement and enthusiasm over the years have enabled me to navigate the author journey so far, and the sheer number of people who wanted this book has been incredible. I shall endeavor to keep serving the community in years to come.

Thanks to my production team: Liz Dexter at LibroEditing, Jane Dixon Smith at JD Smith Design, and thanks to Alexandra Amor and Ellen Bard for beta-reading. Thanks to author Emma Foster for the quote in 1.13.

Lightning Source UK Ltd.
Milton Keynes UK
UKHW020954100720
366327UK00013B/1504

9 781912 105595